WITHDRAWN

Residential Children's Homes and the
Youth Justice System

Residential Children's Homes and the Youth Justice System

Identity, Power and Perceptions

Julie Shaw
Research Fellow, University of Strathclyde, Scotland

palgrave
macmillan

First published 2014 by
PALGRAVE MACMILLAN

Palgrave Macmillan in the UK is an imprint of Macmillan Publishers Limited, registered in England, company number 785998, of Houndmills, Basingstoke, Hampshire RG21 6XS.

Palgrave Macmillan in the US is a division of St Martin's Press LLC, 175 Fifth Avenue, New York, NY 10010.

Palgrave Macmillan is the global academic imprint of the above companies and has companies and representatives throughout the world.

Palgrave® and Macmillan® are registered trademarks in the United States, the United Kingdom, Europe and other countries

ISBN: 978–1–137–31960–9

This book is printed on paper suitable for recycling and made from fully managed and sustained forest sources. Logging, pulping and manufacturing processes are expected to conform to the environmental regulations of the country of origin.

A catalogue record for this book is available from the British Library.

A catalog record for this book is available from the Library of Congress.

Transferred to Digital Printing in 2014

Contents

Part III   Conclusion

Acknowledgements

So many people have helped me in different ways with the research presented here that it is impossible to thank them all. However, I would like to express my thanks to Leeds Metropolitan University for providing the funding which enabled the study to take place. Dr Dorothy Moss, Professor Nick Frost and Dr Jon Tan provided invaluable guidance and encouragement throughout.

I would also like to thank Professor David Berridge (University of Bristol) and Professor Colin Webster (Leeds Metropolitan University) for their helpful comments on various aspects of the research. My appreciation also goes to Jim Wade (University of York) for his guidance during the data collection stages of the project. I am also grateful to the reviewer who commented on the draft proposal of this book and the completed manuscript.

On a personal note, I would like to express my warmest thanks to family and friends who helped and encouraged me in many ways throughout the research process.

Finally, I am particularly grateful to the young people and professionals who gave me their valuable time to both participate in and facilitate the research. Their willingness to talk openly about their experiences and perspectives made the study worthwhile, and my hope is that this research will have a positive impact upon the lives of both current and future children and young people in care.

Introduction

Although children's homes have long been recognised as a potentially 'criminogenic' environment (Hayden, 2010), relatively few studies have specifically addressed why young people in residential care are over-represented in the youth justice system. This book will explore the reasons why young people in residential children's homes come to the attention of the youth justice system, and the consequent implications for policy and practice. I initially decided to undertake this research because while working for a Youth Offending Team, I found that a notable minority of the young people passing through the Youth Court resided in either local authority children's homes, or any number of smaller, private units, which had set up business in the local area over the past few years. Indeed, Ward and Skuse (2001) note that young people who acquired a criminal record after admission to care were significantly more likely to have been living in a residential unit at some point, and in their influential study of 223 children in 48 different children's homes, Sinclair and Gibbs (1998) found that 40 per cent of young people with no cautions or convictions prior to entering care had one after six months or more of living in a children's home. More recently, an Executive Summary of research findings published by The Adolescent and Children's Trust (TACT) in 2008, states that, 'residential care was highlighted in both the literature and in the practitioner survey as the care setting which posed by far the greatest risk to young people in terms of criminalisation' (p.2), something which was confirmed by Darker, Ward and Caulfield (2008). In addition, recent figures reveal that the rate of offending amongst children in residential care was 21.4 per cent compared to 3.6 per cent in foster care and approximately 3 per cent for all children and young people (Nacro, 2012).

Consideration of why this might be the case is particularly relevant at a time when efforts are being made to improve outcomes in the residential care sector in the wake of the 'Care Matters' process (DfES, 2006; DfES, 2007), and important given that research has shown that young people are more likely to choose residential care over foster care (Sinclair and Gibbs, 1998). Indeed, recent research undertaken as part of the former DCSF's *Quality Protects* research initiative found that most young people were very positive about the residential care they received and generally felt safe where they were living. The quality of care provided was also assessed as positive by the researchers and many residents showed improvement on general measures of behavioural, emotional and social difficulties and education (Berridge et al., 2008). Berridge, Biehal and Henry (2012, p.6) assert that 'these results suggest that children's residential care might have the potential to make a more positive contribution' and certainly, Smith (2009a, p.165) argues that residential care has the potential to be 'a conducive environment for children to grow up in', providing that a 'fundamental rethink of the discourses that currently shape policy and practice' takes place.

In countries such as Denmark, Germany, the Netherlands and France, outcomes for children in residential care are generally far better than those in England, although there is disagreement as to whether this is because the different management practices and approaches used in these countries achieve better outcomes, or simply because children with the most serious problems are concentrated in English homes (Hannon, Wood and Bazalgette, 2010). Certainly, as will be discussed throughout the book, it is apparent that while pre-care experiences and the individual disposition of young people have a part to play in terms of their likelihood of youth justice involvement, the available evidence also suggests that other factors directly connected to the experience of being in residential care, have the potential to significantly impact upon outcomes, in both positive and negative ways. These include the influence of the resident group (Sinclair and Gibbs, 1998; Stewart et al., 1994; Emond, 2003; Barter, 2008 and Morgan, 2009), staff-resident relationships (King, Raynes and Tizard, 1973; Whitaker, Archer and Hicks, 1998;

Clough, 2000 and Berridge, 2002), the culture and characteristics of the homes (Whitaker, Archer and Hicks, 1998; Sinclair and Gibbs, 1998; Berridge and Brodie, 1998; Brown et al., 1998; Anglin, 2002 and Hicks et al., 2007) and placement movement (Munro and Hardy, 2007). The question of to what degree these factors are significant is an important one, especially given the tendency of policy and practice within both the care and youth justice contexts to 'individualise' troublesome and offending behaviour and responses to it (see Goldson, 2002; Smith, 2009a, p.12), with an emphasis being placed upon young people taking responsibility for their own actions and responsibility for change. An example of this can be found in the increasing popularity of restorative justice techniques to tackle troublesome behaviour in children's homes (see Willmott, 2007). The emphasis of such initiatives is primarily upon the young person taking responsibility for their actions and making appropriate amends, which, while clearly beneficial in certain respects, does not take into account the wider complexity of factors which might have contributed to their behaviour and will therefore only ever be a partial solution. The need to raise awareness of such factors and how they might best be ameliorated is crucial in terms of determining how policy and practice should be developed in order to achieve improved outcomes for young people, and is the primary aim of this book. Only in this way can we hope to make realistic progress towards addressing involvement in the youth justice system in a way which will be of benefit to the greatest number of children and young people.

Terminology

In accordance with the definition incorporated into the Children Act 1989 and the United Nations Convention on the Rights of the Child (1989), the terms 'child' or 'children' are used to refer to all individuals under the age of 18. However, when discussing the older children (aged 15 to 17) and young adults who are the subject of this book, the terms 'young person' or 'young people' will also be used.

A further issue is how we refer to children and young people who live within the care system. In the United Kingdom two terms tend to be used: these are either 'in care', or 'looked-after' children and young people, sometimes abbreviated to LAC (looked-after children).

The Children Act 1989 introduced the term 'looked-after' as a less stigmatising replacement for the term 'in care', yet the latter continues to dominate in wider society, with the former being applied mainly in official/professional circles (Taylor, 2006). Throughout this book, the terms 'children in care' and 'young people in care' are primarily used.

In addition, while recognising the wide variety of residential care provision, the study did not focus upon the experiences of individuals who require it as the result of some form of disability or those who are accommodated in secure units. The terms 'children's home' or 'residential unit' are used to refer to mainstream residential placements which accommodate children and young people in care and are operated either by local authorities, private companies or voluntary sector organisations.

Research themes and participants

Through a series of semi-structured interviews and documentary data analysis, the study drew upon the direct experiences and perspectives of 12 current and former young people in care aged between 15 and 22, who had previously come to the attention of the youth justice system whilst resident in either local authority or private residential children's homes in a case study area in the north of England, referred to as 'Coalton'. It explored the significance of their experiences both prior and subsequent to entering residential care, and considered the impact of factors at an individual, institutional and wider-systemic (policy and practice) level upon youth justice involvement and the potential for criminalization. Throughout Chapters 4–7, quotations from the young people are used to illustrate points made in the text and are referenced by a pseudonym, followed by the age of the respondent at interview – for example, 'Robbie, 17'.

While recognising the importance of the young people's perceptions, it is also the case that their experiences whilst in residential care can be significantly shaped by the professionals with whom they come into contact; as such, an understanding of their motivations and perceptions is invaluable. Consequently, through a series of semi-structured interviews and a focus group, responses from the professional groups within the care and youth justice systems were also sought. These included social workers, children's home staff and managers, leaving care workers, youth offending team workers (YOT), magistrates, legal advisers, solicitors and police officers. Particular attention was paid to how the underlying perceptions of social workers and residential care staff impact upon their actions and the consequent experiences of the young people. Again, quotations are used to illustrate points made in text and are referenced by the professionals' job title. A broader discussion of the research strategy and methods can be found in Chapter 3.

Uniquely for a study about offending in residential children's homes, the findings were analysed with reference to the concepts of identity formation; reputation (the quest for 'social recognition'); and power (or lack thereof) at the individual, institutional and wider-systemic levels and these themes will be in evidence throughout the book. As explored in Chapter 3, an eclectic range of theoretical perspectives which seek to analyse human behaviour at those levels were utilised, along with a wide range of empirical research. The findings will be discussed with reference to recent policy and practice initiatives in the care and youth justice fields, with suggestions made regarding how outcomes might be improved in the future.

Objectives of the book

Following on from the previous sections, the objectives of the book are to:

- Highlight and analyze the factors at individual, institutional and systemic (over-arching policy and practice) levels which contribute to young people in residential children's homes coming to the attention of the youth justice system.
- Highlight the degree to which such factors are pertinent.
- Examine how the attitudes, perceptions and subsequent actions of professionals can contribute to the experiences of the young people and consequent criminalization.
- Make recommendations for policy and practice based upon the research findings.

This book is highly relevant to professionals in the care and youth justice systems who work with young people in residential care, as well as those responsible for policy development in these arenas. Its interdisciplinary themes mean that it is also applicable to academics and students of Social Work, Childhood and Youth Studies, Criminology, Sociology, Social Policy, Social History, Youth Justice, and Criminal Justice, discussing both relevant theory and practice. The book aims to make a useful contribution to the relatively limited body of knowledge in this area.

The layout of the book

In order to appreciate the context of contemporary residential care and the consequent experiences of children and young people, it is necessary to understand the developments which have influenced policy and practice in this area. The first chapter thus embarks upon a discussion of the history of English residential care up to and including the present day, considering the numerous factors which have contributed to the nature of provision on offer. This is followed by a discussion of what existing research tells us about why individuals might come to the attention of the youth justice system and then a critical analysis of current responses to offending in residential care. Chapter 2 then goes on to consider the impact upon those in children's homes of seemingly contradictory policy initiatives which have attempted to improve the experiences and outcomes of both individuals in care and, more generally, children and young people who are disadvantaged, and those aimed at young people who offend or who are considered to be at risk of doing so. Chapter 3 introduces the research study by advancing the theoretical framework which informed and underpinned it, before outlining the research strategy and methods adopted in relation to the empirical work upon which subsequent chapters are based. The next four chapters detail, discuss and critically analyse the research findings, starting with an exploration of the reasons why children and young people begin to get into trouble and the implications that this has for future offending in the residential care context, and a consideration of professional perceptions of responsibility for challenging behaviour (Chapter 4). Chapter 5 covers perceptions of how troublesome behaviour can be precipitated and influenced by factors within the residential context, while Chapter 6 explores how certain aspects of the overall policy framework and system arrangements pertaining to the care system relate to and influence offending behaviour. Chapter 7 explores a number of important questions surrounding the management of residential home based challenging behaviour, before discussing how individuals are viewed by the youth court when prosecuted for such incidents and how care status might impact upon experiences and outcomes. Finally, Chapter 8 considers the conclusions that can be drawn from the study, before making recommendations for policy and future practice.

Part I
Setting the Scene

1
Developments and Experiences in Residential Care

A historical perspective

In common with the pathways and development of residential child care in different countries of the world (Courtney, Tolev and Gilligan, 2009), it is important to recognise that the nature of English provision and subsequent outcomes have invariably been influenced by a number of interconnected factors. These include: the socio-economic status of those who have required assistance and related ideas regarding the causes of poverty and the nature of the poor; theoretical developments and cultural norms concerning the best ways to parent children; scandals of abuse and the resultant enquiries and financial and political considerations. It will be seen throughout the book that such factors continue to exert a powerful influence on perceptions, policy and practice, and the consequent experiences of children and young people. This is particularly important to bear in mind when considering why residents of children's homes might come to the attention of the youth justice system.

Frost, Mills and Stein (1999) provide a detailed historical account of the attempts of the state to regulate the perceived threat posed by the poor and the dispossessed, with specific provision for children and young people beginning to emerge by 1536. There was an emerging emphasis on child welfare, with the establishment in 1552 of charitable residential provision aimed specifically at children: the key aim of Christ's Hospital was ensuring that children were educated and able to pursue a trade. According to Frost, Mills and Stein (1999, p.8), these developments represented, 'an educative model which was designed to train and crucially rescue children from a future of vagrancy'. However, there was a 'coercive back-up' for this educative ideal, with those who attempted to run away being punished and deprived of their liberty. Indeed, the presence of a 'coercive back-up' has often been a feature of provision for children and young people in the position of being reliant upon the state or charitable provision:

> What we have seen is the inherent tension between 'care' and 'control'-an expressed wish to improve the condition of pauperised children and young people, which exists side by side with punishment, control and containment. (ibid., p.10)

As will become apparent throughout the book, the 'care' and 'control' dichotomy continues to exert a powerful influence upon the experiences of young people in residential children's homes, arguably even more so in current times given that such provision is now generally reserved for those who are perceived to be the most challenging in the system.

When the Industrial Revolution brought about social and economic upheaval, with the rural poor migrating to urban centres, attention focused on the control of what were perceived to be the 'dangerous classes'. This, in turn, had an impact upon the way that their children were perceived and responded to, producing a shift to more punitive attitudes. In 1834, the Poor Law Amendment Act led to a growth in the number of residential establishments, most of which were 'multi-purpose' workhouses where all paupers were housed together. Workhouses operated in accordance with the principle of 'less eligibility', which came about as part of a widespread concern over the able-bodied unemployed, who were often perceived as being the authors of their own misfortunes: lazy and unwilling to earn enough money to support themselves. As a result of this, it was considered that they should be encouraged to seek work and provide for themselves, by ensuring that workhouse conditions were such that only the desperate would seek its assistance, thus producing regimes which enforced harsh and petty rules and regulations. Smith describes how, 'the Poor Laws thus embedded punitive and negative images of the poor, in which poverty was individualized and considered in isolation of the social context from which it stemmed' (2009a, p.21).

While the official dominance of the 'less eligibility' principle ended in the early twentieth century, when, 'a number of surveys and reports pointed to the widespread nature of poverty and suggested that the causes lay outside of individual failure and pathology' (Frost, Mills and Stein, 1999, pp.18–19), it is apparent that in many respects such perceptions of the poor remain embedded in the public consciousness. This is evidenced by the very recent discourse regarding the 'deserving' and 'undeserving' poor surrounding the reform of welfare benefits being undertaken at the time of writing by the UK Coalition government and, indeed, Jackson (2006, p.11) highlights how:

> Long after workhouses – at least under that name – had disappeared, the idea of 'less eligibility', that provision for children in care should never be better than they might of enjoyed in their family and class of origin, maintained a strong influence on the thinking of policy makers and administrators.

Residential children's homes in England continue to be used almost exclusively for children from socially disadvantaged backgrounds and certainly, such attitudes were in evidence amongst some of the care system professionals in this research, when they expressed a concern that young people should not be given unrealistic expectations of the 'reality' of life after leaving care by the provision of too generous an allowance or too many expensive outings or holidays. Such ideas feed into an unhelpfully limited view of what young people in care can achieve and if unchallenged will continue to be a barrier to improved outcomes.

Nevertheless, 'the aftermath of the Second World War and the acknowledgement of the disruption of family life caused by evacuation prompted social reformers to take stock of provision for children' (Smith, 2009a, p.25). The death of a child, Dennis O'Neill, beaten and starved to death in 1945 in a foster home which was subject to only cursory inspection, coincided with this and further galvanised calls for reform. The Curtis Report of 1946 set out the basic form of the present English care system and the principles underlying it, including the ideal of bringing up each child in a way resembling as closely as possible ordinary family life. It was critical of large-scale institutional living and proposed that children and young people should be provided for in smaller units (of around 20 children) located nearer to centres of population. The report laid great emphasis on the need to treat each child/young person as an individual, in contrast to the institutional nature of most child care at the time and, 'came down firmly in favour of foster care as preferable to children's homes, urging local authorities to make a "vigorous effort" to extend the system' (Jackson, 2006, p.13). Smith (2009a) highlights how the child guidance movement, drawing on Freudian psychology and emphasising the importance of working with children in the context of their family relationships, was a powerful influence on the thinking of the time. Nevertheless, children and young people continued to be accommodated primarily in institutional settings for a number of years.

The subsequent Children Act 1948 established local authority children's departments as the first professional social work service for children and young people in the United Kingdom. The departments ran their own residential establishments and employed fostering and adoption officers to find families for orphaned, neglected and abused children and young people. Section 12(1) of the Act states that:

> Where a child is in the care of a local authority it shall be the duty of that authority to exercise their powers with respect to him so as to further his best interests; and to afford him opportunity for the proper development of his character and abilities.

Here, there appears to be legislative acknowledgement that, in theory at least, the child in care is an individual with a distinct personality and needs, rather than belonging to a homogenous group which requires management and control. As later described, these sentiments have been reiterated and further enshrined in subsequent legislation and policy. However, as will be illustrated throughout this book, it is arguable that in many respects and for a number of reasons, local authorities still struggle to fulfil such aspirations, to the continuing detriment of young people, particularly in residential care.

During the 1950s and 1960s, the Family Group Home became the favoured unit for the long term placement of children and young people, designed to reflect the 'conventional' family as far as possible. However, it could be argued that the primary development of this period was the challenge to the residential institution which came from the research of John Bowlby (1953). Bowlby's highly influential theory of maternal deprivation suggested that disturbed or delinquent behaviour by children and young people was the result of the lack of consistent and adequate mothering during their early years. It was thus considered that the residential environment could not provide the attachment relationships that children need to thrive. Frost, Mills and Stein (1999, p.22) describe how, as well as being consistent with the official preference for fostering, which was favoured as being closer to a 'normal' upbringing, the research, 'also coincided with the concern of the social democratic consensus to break with the Poor Law, which was symbolised by institutionalised forms of care' (ibid., p.22). The official attitude towards residential provision was further reinforced by the findings of research undertaken by Goffman (1961), which was heavily critical of the impact of institutions upon their inmates. Alongside such developments, in the 1960s the emphasis moved towards maintaining children within their families wherever possible with the Children and Young Person's Act 1963 giving local authorities the duty to provide assistance to families in order to keep children out of care.

It is also of note that 'until the early 1970s the care population included many young offenders, who were placed in residential homes by the courts and typically remained there for two years' (Berridge, Biehal and Henry, 2012, p.3). However, the Children and Young Person's Act 1969 focused on alternatives to custody and led to a decline in the use of community homes with education for this purpose, a trend which was further reinforced by the Children Act 1989, which ended the use of care orders as a disposal for young offenders. Consequently, 'a significant group of young people previously placed in residential homes as a result of their offending disappeared from the care system' (ibid., p.3). It is undoubtedly the case that this use of residential care further reinforced the stigma attached to placement in a children's home, a stigma which has continued to endure.

Nonetheless, Sinclair and Gibbs (1998) argue that the research basis which fuelled the disapproval of residential care was unsound, given that Goffman's work was heavily influenced by a study of one psychiatric institution and Bowlby's by the studies of a kind of orphanage which England no longer has. However, 'the impact of this research was then to help to establish a clear hierarchy of child placement-adoption, fostering and, least desirable, residential care' (Frost, Mills and Stein, 1999, p.22). Such attitudes later became further entrenched by a series of abuse scandals which came to light in the 1990s, and were investigated in a series of inquiries and reports (see for example Warner, 1992; Waterhouse, 2000). Concerns regarding cost have also played a part, particularly in connection with the doctrine of managerialism introduced to the public services in the 1980s by Margaret Thatcher's 'New Right' Conservatives, and its watchwords of 'economy, efficiency and effectiveness' (Smith, 2009a, p.7). In 2011 the weekly cost of care in a local authority children's home was estimated at £2767 per week, compared with an average cost of £694 for foster care (DfE, 2012a), although Berridge, Biehal and Henry (2012) point out that the cost of specialist foster placements for young people with similar levels of need to those placed in children's homes is likely to be considerably higher. Consequently, contemporary residential children's homes are seen very much as residual provision for the most challenging children and young people, staffed by a largely unqualified workforce (Berridge, Biehal and Henry, 2012; Cliffe and Berridge, 1991). This is despite the fact that, 'research findings do not indicate that alternative interventions are demonstrably superior' (Berridge and Brodie, 1998, p.22) and that 'for many young people... good residential care is not a last resort, but rather a preferred and positive choice when their developmental challenges indicate the need for it' (Anglin and Knorth, 2004, p.141).

Residential care today

In response to the ideological swing against interventionism, the number of children in care in England has fallen significantly over the past thirty years, from 92,000 in 1981 to 54, 000 in 1998 (House of Commons Health Select Committee, 1998; Fawcett, Featherstone and Goddard, 2004, p.76), to 68,110 in the year ending 31 March 2013 (DfE, 2013c). Children in England are now overwhelmingly placed in foster care, which has become more professionalised and currently accounts for 75 per cent of all care placements (DfE, 2013c). In common with Australia, the USA and Canada, the use of residential provision in England has declined substantially, accounting in 2013 for approximately 9 per cent of placements (DfE, 2013c – this statistic encompasses children's homes, secure units and hostels), the proportion having decreased steadily from 32 per cent in 1978 (Berridge, Biehal and Henry, 2012). This is low by comparison with some other European Union countries: in Denmark, France and the Netherlands, there is a more equal balance of foster and residential care provision and in Southern, Central and Eastern Europe, residential care is predominant (Kendrick, Steckley and McPheat, 2011).

Over the last 30 years there has been a decline in the in-house provision of residential care by local authorities; at the time of writing, 52 out of 152 local authorities do not operate any homes and ten do not have any children's homes at all in their areas (DfE, 2013a). Almost half have closed at least one of their children's homes since 2008. As local authorities have moved towards commissioning more placements from the independent sector, particularly from larger providers of children's homes (Pemberton, 2011), the latest figures for England indicate that 1,718 children's homes were registered with Ofsted on 31 March 2013 and that of these, 371 (22 per cent) were local authority run and 1,347 (78 per cent) were in the private or voluntary sector. To place such figures in context, this represents a 39 per cent reduction in local authority provision from 61 per cent in 2000 (DfE, 2013a).

Berridge, Biehal and Henry (2012, p.5) state that 'it seems likely that this trend will continue, as at least 17 per cent of local authorities recently informed Community Care magazine that they plan to close at least one residential home or are reviewing their service'. This can result in young people being placed out of area away from family and friends, which while at times beneficial in safe-guarding terms and/or the provision of specialist services, may also include further disruption of schooling, difficulties regarding the provision of health care and the potential to cause distress at the loss of previously formed attachments resulting in concomitant behavioural difficulties. There is also the important question of whether private provision is able to meet the needs of such young people or whether, as has been the case in other sectors (Scourfield, 2007), income generation will be prioritised over quality of care.

Nevertheless, in what can be seen as something of a sea-change in terms of government rhetoric, recent pronouncements have seemingly reflected the growing body of research which has cast residential care in a more positive light (e.g. Sinclair and Gibbs, 1998;

Emond, 2003; Anglin and Knorth, 2004; Berridge et al., 2008). The *Care Matters* White Paper (Department for Education and Skills, 2007, p.57) which was the precursor to the Children and Young Person's Act 2008, acknowledged that residential care has an important role to play as part of a range of placement options, but again endorsed foster and kinship care (where children are placed with family members or unrelated people who are in the child's social network), as the ideal for the majority, thereby retaining the status quo. The Conservative-Liberal Democrat Coalition government elected in 2010, also agreed that residential care can make a significant contribution to good quality placement choice for young people, but in addition stated that, 'local authorities should see residential care as a positive placement option to meet a child's needs rather than as a last resort where fostering placements break down' (House of Commons, 2011). After decades where theoretical, ideological and political objections to residential care have stymied its use, this appears to be a significant step forward in acknowledging the positive potential of such provision at government level. However, given the financial cost of this resource in comparison with mainstream foster care, it will remain to be seen whether the political will truly exists to support its emergence as anything other than a residual service. Indeed, in times of austerity such as those currently being experienced in the UK, it seems highly unlikely that local authorities already making cuts to services and endeavouring to balance more limited budgets, will be encouraged to reverse their decisions to close existing children's homes or to place more young people in residential placements, whether operated by the public, private or voluntary sector. As a consequence of this, it is likely that the current state of affairs will endure.

The link between residential care and offending

When considering why young people in children's homes might come to the attention of the youth justice system, it is first useful to consider what can be gleaned from existing research studies and other available data. A useful starting point is to consider the reasons individuals are taken into care and the implications that this might have for future behaviour. Children and young people can be voluntarily accommodated under section 20 of the 1989 Children Act. Here their parents continue to have parental responsibility and, in theory at least, should play a major role whilst their children are accommodated. A further percentage is placed away from home under an emergency protection order or on police protection/remand/detention (section 21 of the 1989 Children Act). However, the majority become looked-after under the auspices of a compulsory Care Order in accordance with section 31 of the Act, having suffered or being at risk of suffering likely 'significant harm' attributable to the care given or likely to be given. Here, the local authority assumes parental responsibility, shared with the child's parents. In this context, 'harm' may include being considered at risk of involvement in criminal activity. Although it is no longer possible to make a care order on the grounds of criminal proceedings, individuals may be placed on a care order if they are considered to be 'beyond parental control'. Consequently, such young people may be exhibiting antisocial behaviour, even if they have not yet committed or been found guilty of a criminal offence and could therefore be at risk of continuing such behaviour when in care. In the year ending 31 March 2013, 59 per cent of children and young people in care were the subject of full or interim Care Orders and 27 per cent were voluntarily accommodated under section 20 (DfE, 2013c).

Following on from this, there is little doubt that a reason for youth justice involvement amongst those in residential care can be found in the fact that almost all children in care are, 'from backgrounds of deprivation, poor parenting, abuse and neglect-factors that together are risk factors for a range of emotional, social and behavioural difficulties, including anti-social and offending behaviour' (Schofield et al., 2012, p.1). Indeed, due to the residual nature of UK residential care, the individuals placed in children's homes are generally older (mostly over the age of 12), vulnerable and more likely to have complex needs and serious difficulties. They are also more likely to have been through many care placements (APPG, 2012; DfE, 2012a; Berridge et al., 2008) and have moved there either from home or from foster care as a result of their challenging behaviour (Berridge, Biehal and Henry, 2012). Although less likely to be the primary reason they are looked after than for those in other placements (62 per cent in the overall looked-after population, DfE, 2013c), recent statistics indicate that 44 per cent of children's home residents nevertheless entered care for reasons of abuse and neglect (DfE, 2012a) and indeed, there is evidence some young people may have experienced abuse or neglect which was unidentified prior to admission (Biehal, 2005; Stein et al., 2009). Other reasons include family dysfunction (18 per cent), family in acute stress (14 per cent) and socially unacceptable behaviour (6 per cent) (DfE, 2012a). Of course, there may be elements of overlap in the categories; for example, while a young person may have been abused or neglected, they might also have been exhibiting a degree of socially unacceptable behaviour.

Therefore, whilst few individuals are actually admitted to care under criminal proceedings, many may enter care because they are already regarded as at risk of involvement in crime. In addition, poor quality parenting and maltreatment may 'impact upon their coping skills, including the ability to act appropriately, express themselves adequately and to conform to social norms' (Nacro, 2012), which means that they will run a high risk of getting into trouble regardless of where they are placed. Certainly, the majority of young people spend only relatively short periods of time in care and as will be expanded upon in the following chapter, it has been argued that poor outcomes often cannot be separated from negative pre-care experiences (Stein, 2006). Indeed, in their study of 16 children's homes across the public, private and voluntary sectors, Berridge, Biehal and Henry (2012) found that two-thirds of the young people in their study had been in trouble with the police during the previous six months and that the 'adolescent entrants' to care (those who enter at the age of 11 or over) were significantly more likely to have been in trouble with the police than the 'graduates' (those who become looked after before the age of 11 years and grow up in care) of the care system (63 per cent and 38 per cent respectively). Darker, Ward and Caulfield (2008) examined the association between local authority care and offending behaviour in 250 young people of the age of criminal responsibility and found that overall, being in care did not appear to be associated with a significant increase in the rate of offending; they conclude that for those who did offend, the care episode itself was unlikely to have been the sole cause of their delinquency.

Nevertheless, there is also significant evidence to suggest that the backgrounds of the young people do not tell the full story regarding why they might get into trouble (Sinclair and Gibbs, 1998; Waterhouse, 2000) and indeed, in the postscript to his report on the abuse of children in care in Gwynedd and Clwyd, Waterhouse (2000) remarked that care homes had been notably unsuccessful in terms of crime prevention. It emerged that 52 complainants had convictions prior to entering care, but 85 were convicted of offences whilst in care. Waterhouse concluded that, 'some children who had not offended before were introduced to delinquency and to harsh regimes in which they were treated by some staff as "little criminals" ... some regimes encouraged absconsion and increased offending' (Waterhouse, 2000, p.840). Darker, Ward and Caulfield (2008) highlight how qualitative data from interviews with young people who had left care suggested that offending behaviour was more common in certain residential homes than in other placements. They ascribe this partly to the fact that in some residential units, a culture which tended to criminalise children and young people had developed. This has been a long-standing cause for concern and many sources have identified a particularly low threshold reported by some young people for police involvement in children's homes (Fitzpatrick, 2009; Nacro, 2003, 2005, 2012; Morgan, 2006) often as a result of incidents which would in all likelihood not have been brought to official attention if the resident had lived in a family home.

Darker, Ward and Caulfield (2008) also ascribe offending behaviour to the fact that the persistent or prolific offenders in their study were more likely to be placed eventually in residential units. This clearly increases the likelihood that such young people might continue to offend, but also has implications in terms of their ability to influence those who might have little or no previous youth justice involvement. Indeed, Taylor (2006, p.88) argues that, 'the "university of crime" concept may be applicable to certain residential care units, particularly in explaining how residents pick up criminal "skills" regardless of whether they have previously been in trouble or not'. The potential influence of the peer culture upon offending in residential care should therefore be carefully considered. However, this should be balanced against other research which has found that support and help from young people, getting to know young people from different backgrounds and having other children and young people to share interests and activities with were important to many and considered to be some of the best things about living in a children's home (Morgan, 2009; Emond, 2003) and could potentially mitigate against poor outcomes.

A further factor for consideration lies in the acknowledged variability of the quality of care provided by residential children's homes and how this might impact upon subsequent behaviour. Outcomes have been found to be strongly linked to the individual cultures and characteristics of homes (Whitaker, Archer and Hicks, 1998; Sinclair and Gibbs, 1998; Berridge and Brodie, 1998; Brown et al., 1998; Hicks et al., 2007; Anglin, 2002) with research stressing the importance of 'leadership in developing positive cultures in residential care' (Kendrick, Steckley and McPheat, 2011, p.296), including a high degree of congruence between policy, organisational, unit and individual goals (Brown et al., 1998). Residential workers have often been found to be more reactive than proactive, responding to children's problems rather than creating solutions (Colton, 1988; Berridge and Brodie, 1988). King, Raynes and Tizard (1973), Whitaker, Archer and Hicks (1998), Clough (2000) and Berridge (2002) emphasise that results in children's homes are best where children are accorded respect as individuals and effective relationships built between staff and young people, which take into account the children's perspective. In addition, two contemporaneous studies found that more effective homes tended to be small, thus helping to reduce problems in managing individual behaviour and group dynamics (Sinclair and Gibbs, 1998; Berridge and Brodie, 1998). Nevertheless, the question of what 'small' should ideally mean in order to produce the best outcomes is something which has proved to be contentious and will be discussed at a later point. Another study found that going missing was far more widespread in residential care than in foster care and, in many cases, residents committed offences while they were absent. This was associated with the pre-placement histories of the young people, but also with environmental factors, specifically the placement culture (Biehal and Wade, 2000).

Overall therefore, there are a number of disparate elements which have the potential to contribute to behavioural outcomes and consequent police involvement in residential care. These elements, which include the individual pre-care experiences of the young people and the nature of available provision in what has become a residual service, will be investigated further in the forthcoming chapters.

Current responses to offending in residential care

Offending whilst resident in a children's home can take place in a variety of contexts and locations, including the home itself, out in the wider community or while visiting family. However, the inappropriate criminalisation through police and court involvement as a response to challenging behaviour or minor offending committed on the premises of children's homes is 'one of the main concerns about the placement of young people in residential care' (Nacro, 2012, p.21). This has often been exacerbated by punitive and interventionist developments in youth justice policy since the 1990s, many of which will be discussed in the following chapter.

Nevertheless, there has been a growing awareness of the need for strategies to manage these incidents in a proportionate way, and Children's Home National Minimum Standards 2011 Section 3.22 (DfE, 2012b) require that a home's approach to care minimises the need for police involvement to deal with challenging behaviour and avoids criminalising children unnecessarily. A number of approaches have emerged which include developing protocols and relationships with the police for the reporting of offending, promoting positive behaviour strategies in the placement and using restorative approaches which can help residential staff to respond to incidents (Nacro, 2012)

The Children Act 1989 Guidance and Regulations (Volume 5): Children's Homes (DfE, 2013b), states that children should not be charged with offences resulting from behaviour which would not lead to police involvement if it occurred in a family home (2.85). This is also advocated by a Home Office report on young people in local authority residential care (HO, 2004), which proceeds to advise that a further consideration should be whether there is a real threat to the safety of other residents or staff. The report concludes that protocols with the police would be beneficial in achieving considerable reductions in reported incidents and offences, and would encourage staff to take the following into consideration:

- The context of the incident and what might be an appropriate response.
- How difficult behaviour should be managed.
- How to respond more consistently to certain types of incidents.
- The development of restorative approaches to problematic behaviour.

(Nacro, 2012, p.22)

Nacro (2012) argues that making a clear distinction between problematic behaviour and criminal behaviour is clearly a starting point:

> Children's home providers should establish a presumption that, wherever possible, efforts will be made to address problematic behaviour through professional help and support and without recourse to the criminal justice system unless absolutely necessary. (ibid., p.21)

It is reported that a number of local authority areas have developed protocols for this purpose (including one between Bradford Police, Bradford YOT and Children's Social Care and others between relevant local authorities and Sussex, Hampshire and Staffordshire police forces) (Nacro, 2012) and in the case study area that is the subject of this book, a protocol had been in place for approximately 18 months at the time the research was undertaken. Schofield et al. (2012) argue that protocols for managing offending in children's homes are most likely to be effective when there is also a positive working relationship with police officers, where protocols and liaison with the police are readily accepted and where training on restorative approaches to incidents in children's homes has been fully provided. The question of whether such good intentions are translating into effective practice and issues surrounding the management of challenging behaviour in children's homes are explored in greater detail in Chapter 7.

In addition to such protocols, the use of restorative approaches in children's homes is currently regarded as a good way of preventing the escalation or repetition of difficult behaviour and providing an informal way of resolving problems that might otherwise be reported to the police (Willmott, 2007; Littlechild and Sender, 2010). The aim of such approaches is to encourage young people to realise the impact of their offence or behaviour and deter them from similar behaviour in the future. Rather than being punitive in nature, a problem-solving focus is regarded as being most effective. Restorative approaches traditionally work by bringing together the victim (with their consent) and the offender and encouraging a dialogue between the two parties. The victim is thus encouraged to describe the impact of the offence on them, and the offender to explain why they offended and apologise for the damage and distress they caused. The hope is that such an approach will lead to a greater understanding on both sides about the cause and effect of the offending. Littlechild and Sender (2010) suggest that because children's homes are more akin to a domestic environment, where relationships are more intimate and intense and the perpetrator and victim know each other, restorative approaches in residential settings need to be conducted in a different way to those traditionally associated with the criminal justice system. As a result, informality and the development of conflict resolution processes (sometimes described as relational conflict resolution) are used.

Another approach is mediation, which focuses on the resolution of disputes, thus enabling both parties to express their views and to discuss how problems can be resolved. Informal restorative meetings in which a member of staff who has a good rapport with the young person finds ways of enabling them to face up to the consequences of their behaviour, as well as helping them to find a suitable way of making reparation, are a further possibility. In some residential settings, in appropriate circumstances, young people conduct the process with an adult present to mediate if necessary (Littlechild and Sender, 2010).

Littlechild and Sender (2010) highlight that when effectively implemented the use of restorative approaches in children's homes can reduce police call-outs by around a fifth. Although not without some potential difficulties, including those inherent in using restorative approaches with young people who bully others and the possibility that some will simply pay 'lip service' to its principles, they report that working restoratively in children's homes has been found to have a number of beneficial effects:

- It helps young people to learn to manage their anger.
- It gives them a sense of responsibility and guilt.
- It helps them to understand that actions have consequences.
- It is a means of acknowledging the young person and giving them a voice.
- It makes them feel they are part of a process.
- It helps them to develop different responses to different situations.
- It helps them to develop empathy and build relationships.

Nacro (2012) reported that one particular local authority (Norfolk) has instigated training in restorative approaches in its residential units as part of a wider initiative to reduce the number of looked-after children in the youth justice system and to develop better ways of working with children in residential care which in turn has led to the number of young people charged with criminal offences dropping by half over a two-year period. It is argued that 'in order to effectively and systematically deliver restorative approaches, appropriate training must be delivered to all staff in children's homes, both on induction and on a refresher basis' (ibid., p.22).

While such developments appear encouraging, it should not be forgotten that restorative approaches essentially focus upon the deficits of the identified young person. The onus is placed first and foremost upon individuals to accept responsibility for their actions and responsibility for change. As discussed in the previous section and as will be in evidence throughout this book, a whole range of factors at the individual and wider systemic levels, have the potential to contribute to challenging behaviour and bring children to the attention of the police. Therefore, while arguably a useful additional tool for professionals, a focus upon such approaches should not obscure our shared responsibility for the improvement of other factors.

Conclusion

This chapter began by highlighting that throughout its long history, the nature of English residential care provision has been influenced by a range of interconnecting variables, including financial and political considerations; scandals of abuse and subsequent inquiries; ideas regarding the best ways to parent children and the perceived nature of the poor: factors which have at times resulted in a tension between the 'care' and 'control' of young people who are reliant upon the state. Certainly, despite existing research and additional data revealing a number of disparate elements which might potentially contribute to youth justice involvement, the nature of responses to offending in the residential care context have thus far primarily concentrated upon the correction and control of perceived individual deficits. This is clearly far from ideal, failing as it does to consider the contribution of other factors relating to both pre- and in-care experiences.

Indeed, young people in care are often both 'troubled and troublesome' (Goldson, 2002) and it is arguably this dichotomy which has resulted in seemingly contradictory policy in the care and youth justice arenas. The following chapter considers the current policy climate in which this investigation takes place, highlighting the tensions that exist between policy which is intended to improve outcomes for young people in care, and developments in the area of youth justice which have at times run counter to this.

2
Policy Context of Research

The care and control dichotomy

Over recent years, a number of policy initiatives have attempted to improve the experiences and outcomes of both individuals in care and, more generally, children and young people who are disadvantaged via measures aimed at tackling 'social exclusion' and promoting 'social justice'. Alongside this, we have until recently witnessed an increasingly punitive and interventionist stance being taken towards young people who offend or who are considered to be at risk of doing so. Indeed, Goldson refers to the emergence of a 'deserving-undeserving schism' (Goldson, 2002, p.683), whereby the welfare of child offenders is side-lined and they are stigmatised and made the subject of punitive interventions, although it is often the case that (as with those in residential care) 'troubled and troublesome children are invariably... the same' (ibid., p.690). Certainly, this apparent dichotomy appears to be particularly pertinent to those young people in residential care who are amongst the most vulnerable and troubled in the care system and have a greater chance of getting into trouble than both young people in the general population and individuals in other care placements. While the Children Act 1989 would class them as children 'in need', the youth justice system responds to them largely as offenders who should be held to account for their actions and are deserving of punishment. The following chapter will begin by discussing some of the more recent policy initiatives which are directly applicable to young people in residential care, before moving on to consider the potential impact of youth justice policy upon experiences and outcomes.

Child welfare and Quality Protects

The Children Act 1989 and its companion set of regulations and guidance is significant in providing the current legal and regulatory framework for care in England and Wales. The Children and Young Persons Act 2008 interpolates, or on occasions, substitutes additional sections, and will be discussed in due course. Many of the provisions of the Children Act 1989 reflect the obligations contained in the UN Convention on the Rights of the Child, which entered into force in the UK in 1992. It established the principle that the welfare of the child should be the *paramount* consideration in court proceedings relating to their upbringing and that, in contrast to earlier policy, a court should not make a care order unless it is preferable to making no order. Section 22(3) sets out the primary duty of local authorities to safeguard and promote the welfare of children in care, including a particular duty to promote their educational achievement and in acting as good 'corporate parents' to enable each child to achieve their full potential. Under Section 22, local authorities have a duty to ensure that in commissioning services from providers of children's homes they comply with their responsibilities under the Act. The Act also introduced the representations and complaints procedure (Section 26) for young people in care and there is a clear emphasis in Section 22 and in the relevant guidance, on the importance of children in care being consulted by local authorities before decisions are made about them.

The subsequent Utting (1997) review coined the phrase 'Quality Protects', which became the Department of Health's flagship programme for improving the lives of children in need. The Quality Protects programme was launched in 1998 and implemented in 1999, with the aim of transforming the management and delivery of children's social services. The main objectives relevant to children in care were: ensuring secure attachment to appropriate carers; maximising life chances with regard to education, health and social care; enabling care leavers to participate socially and economically in society; promoting the meaningful involvement of users and carers in planning services and tailoring individual packages of care, ensuring effective complaints mechanisms, and the protection of children and young people in regulated services from harm and poor care standards (Fawcett, Featherstone and Goddard, 2004, pp.78–79). In 2001 a new project aimed at reducing offending amongst children in care was added to the list of projects in the Quality Protects programme, seen by some as an important indicator that the government was beginning to pay attention to the link between care and offending. A target was set to reduce the proportion of children aged 10–17 and looked after continuously for at least a year who had received a final warning or conviction by one-third.

Other key features of the programme included an enhanced performance measurement and inspection regime and the greater involvement of local councillors in implementing the underlying philosophy of 'corporate parenting'. The Care Standards Act 2000 supported the introduction of National Minimum Standards for residential child care provision, which were issued in 2002 (revised in 2010), and the Children (Leaving Care) Act 2000 extended local authority responsibilities towards former children in care.

New Labour and 'social justice'

On coming to power in 1997, considerable emphasis was placed by the New Labour government on the significance of securing social justice for children in general, and on 'tackling' child poverty (currently defined as those living in households with an income below 60 per cent of the mean UK income after housing costs) in particular (Goldson and Muncie, 2006). Indeed, child poverty rose from 1.4 million (or 10 per cent) in 1979 to 4.3 million (34 per cent) by 1999/2000 leading the Commission on Social Justice to observe that: 'Britain is not a good place in which to be a child' (cited in Piachaud, 2001, p.446). Consequently, shortly after being elected, the government announced its 'historic aim' (Blair, 1999) to reduce child poverty by a quarter by 2004/2005, halve it by 2010 and eradicate it completely by 2020. Goldson and Muncie (2006, p.212) note that:

> In addressing the challenges presented by the 'anti-child poverty' strategy and the wider 'social inclusion' agenda with regard to children and in addition to increasing child benefits and enhancing

tax credits, an extraordinarily wide-ranging sequence of cross-government initiatives, policy developments and 'modernising' service re-configurations have been introduced. Such reforms cover the full-range of health, social care, education, training and employment services, alongside regeneration and 'neighbourhood renewal' programmes.

The Green Paper *Every Child Matters* (DfES, 2003) further widened the policy focus to all children, building on existing plans to strengthen preventive services. *Every Child Matters: The Next Steps* (2004) stated that the Government's aim for every child, *whatever their background or circumstances* (author's emphasis) was to have the support they need to be healthy, stay safe, enjoy and achieve, make a positive contribution to society (which also encompassed not engaging in anti-social or offending behaviour) and achieve economic well-being. It was stated that organisations involved with providing services to children, from hospitals and schools, to police and voluntary groups, would team up in new ways, sharing information and working together, to protect children and young people from harm and help them to achieve what they want in life.

Subsequently, the Children Act 2004 made significant changes to the way that agencies work together. It defined new Children's Services Authorities, stating that they have a duty to promote co-operation between specified 'relevant partners' to achieve the five *Every Child Matters* outcomes. Local authorities were required to lead an integrated delivery through multi-agency children's trusts and local safeguarding boards; to draw up a single children and young people's plan; to appoint a children's commissioner and director of children's services and to set up a shared database of children, containing information relevant to their welfare.

While undoubtedly well intentioned, such an approach has not been without its critics. For example, it has been argued by many that a number of government initiatives (whether 'anti-poverty', child 'welfare' and/or community regeneration activities) are – at least partly – 'formulated on the basis of correcting individual "deficits", as distinct from addressing profound forms of social and economic polarisation and inequality by way of redistributive strategies' (Goldson and Muncie, 2006, p.213; Goldson and Jamieson, 2002; Hancock, 2006; Piachaud, 2005; Sutherland, Sefton and

Piachaud, 2003; Webster, 2006; White and Cunneen, 2006). It is also the case that the coverage of such initiatives is far from comprehensive despite substantial financial investment. Indeed, such criticisms could arguably also be levelled at recent Coalition government initiatives, including the 'Troubled Families' programme, which are described in the following section.

The Coalition government: 'troubled families' and 'transforming lives'

Newly elected in 2010, the Conservative-Liberal Democrat Coalition government has thus far presided over a period of economic slowdown, social disturbance and financial austerity, which has impacted negatively upon the lives of many children and families in the UK. Following on from New Labour's Child Poverty Act 2010, which established income targets for 2020 and a duty to minimise socioeconomic disadvantage, the Coalition government set out a Child Poverty Strategy (DWP and DfE, 2011) with the stated aim of 'setting out a new approach to tackling poverty and securing social justice' (p.2). Subsequently, in the aftermath of the riots which took place in London in August 2011, the Government published its strategy entitled *Social Justice: Transforming Lives* (DWP, 2012). Both documents emphasised the importance of reducing welfare dependency and supporting people into work through a combination of incentives and consequences, along with the necessity of early intervention in the lives of disadvantaged families. Indeed, the Prime Minister David Cameron later announced (December 2012) that the government was making available £448 million over three years (2012–2015) in a cross-government drive to 'turn around the lives' of 120,000 of the country's most troubled families (DCLG, 2013). 'Troubled families' are defined as households who:

- Are involved in crime and anti-social behaviour,
- Have children not in school,
- Have an adult on out of work benefits,
- Cause high costs to the public purse.

(The Troubled Families programme: Financial framework for the payment-by-results scheme for local authorities: DCLG, 2012)

It was stated that the former head of the Respect Task Force, Louise Casey, would head a new Troubled Families Team based within the Department for Communities and Local Government to drive forward a non-governmental approach to provide expert help to local areas. The government funding is offered to local authorities on a payment-by-results basis when they and their partners achieve success with families and funds 40 per cent of the intervention, with the remaining 60 per cent coming from the council's own budgets. The Government also funds a national network of Troubled Family 'trouble-shooters' in each (upper-tier) local council who operate at a senior level to oversee the programme of action in their area. However, Levitas (2012) has questioned the reliability of figures used as the basis for the programme, stating that they may be substantially lower or higher, possibly as high as 300,000 and goes on to conclude that:

> It is evident, then, from excavating the reports and analyses on which current rhetoric about 120,000 'troubled families' and the costs they impose on society, that the Coalition misrepresents the research background. In the term 'troubled families' it deliberately conflates families experiencing multiple disadvantage and families that cause trouble. The attributed costing's are obscure and certainly open to question. (ibid., p.12)

Nevertheless, in June 2013, the government announced that an additional £200 million would be invested in the scheme to extend it to 400,000 'high risk' families. It was claimed that the initiative is cost effective for all partners with a one-off average investment of £4,500 in work with each family being projected to reduce the annual average cost of dealing with their problems. It is too early to know whether the scheme will reap dividends in terms of improving the lives of children and young people who might otherwise be at risk of being taken into care or indeed whether any of the initiatives undertaken as part of the *Child Poverty* or *Social Justice: Transforming Lives* strategies will be similarly successful. However, such approaches are again open to the charge that they, 'neglect the systemic inequalities that exist within society and therefore fail to address the necessary structural change, which it can be argued is essential to deliver social justice in the UK and tackle the inequalities that are all-pervasive' (Silver, 2012).

Outcomes for children in care

In the event, despite the plethora of policy initiatives it has been generally perceived that outcomes remain poor for those in care. For example, of those children and young people who were looked after continuously for 12 months at 31 March 2013, only 15.3 per cent achieved 5+ GCSE's (or equivalent) at A*–C grades, including English and Mathematics, compared to 58 per cent of their peers (DfE, 2013e). The Children, Schools and Families Select Committee Report on looked-after children (House of Commons, 2011) reported how, in the long term, those who have been in care are over-represented among teenage parents, drug users and prisoners. Research by Worsley (2006) found that 29 per cent of boys and 44 per cent of girls in custody reported having been in care.

However, it should be noted that alternative views to the pervasive negativity regarding outcomes for children in care have been voiced. Indeed, Stein (2006) argues that as most young people will spend only a relatively short period of time in care, the consensus that children in care are failing, and that the system is to blame, is wrong for the majority of individuals. It is argued that poor outcomes often cannot be separated from negative pre-care experiences. Stein (2006) highlights how research studies carried out at the University of York over a number of years show that despite their very poor starting points, some care leavers will successfully 'move on' from care and achieve fulfilment in their personal lives and careers, while a second group will 'survive' quite well, given assistance from skilled leaving-care workers, leaving a third, highly vulnerable group of young people who have a range of complex mental health needs and will require assistance into and during adulthood:

> It is this latter group, representing about 3%–5% of the...care population, who have become identified in the public and professional consciousness as typical of all young people in the care system, and who are driving the reform agenda. (Stein, 2006)

Such assertions have been strengthened by Forrester et al. (2007) who after undertaking a significant overview of the available evidence, including studies that compared outcomes for children and young people who entered care with those for comparable children who did not; studies that looked at the progress of children and young people in care over time and studies that compared adults who had been in care with other adults who had experienced adversity or difficulty, concluded that:

> There was little evidence of the care system having a negative impact on children's welfare. Indeed, the picture suggested the opposite – in the vast majority of studies children's welfare improved. This picture was fairly consistent. The overall pattern leads us to conclude that on the whole care is a positive experience for most children and that it appears to improve or at least not harm their welfare. (ibid., pp.29–30)

A review undertaken by Brodie and Morris (2009) and a study by Cameron et al. (2007) yielded similarly positive results. Nevertheless, while arguing that the view of a care system failing young people is too simplistic, Stein (2006) goes on to acknowledge both that, 'care could be better' and that 'just to "survive" or "struggle" with complex needs is not good enough'. Certainly, Hannon, Wood and Bazalgette (2010, p.70) argue that 'the fact that care could be improved for many children is not incompatible with the idea that overall, care does not seem to be solely responsible for bad outcomes which are often attributed to the system'. This also links to the fact that young people in care are a diverse group with a variety of needs; as previously stated, 'adolescent entrants' to the care system, such as those young people who are typically accommodated in residential care, experience poorer outcomes when compared with adolescent graduates. Indeed, it has been argued that 'there is a vast range in how positive an experience of care can be' (ibid., 2010, pp.70–71), and Ward, Holmes and Soper (2008) found that those with the highest level of need, particularly individuals who displayed emotional or behavioural difficulties and also committed offences, were served least well by the care system. This clearly has implications for those young people who are currently placed in residential care, who often have the most complex needs and turbulent backgrounds and are more likely to come into contact with the youth justice system.

Care Matters

It was in recognition of the popular perception of negative outcomes that the New Labour government's Green Paper *Care Matters* was published in 2006 (DfES, 2006). Referring to government activity aimed at improving state care in the foreword to the Green Paper, then Secretary of State for Education and Skills, Alan Johnson MP, stated:

> Quite simply it is now clear that this help has not been sufficient. The life chances of all children have been improved but those of children in care have not improved at the same rate. The result is that children in care are now at greater risk of being left behind than was the case a few years ago-the gap has actually grown. (DfES, 2006, p.3)

In some respects the *Care Matters* programme reiterated existing ideals. It was again asserted that corporate parents' aspirations for children and young people in care should be exactly the same as any parents' aspirations for their own child and a strengthening of the inspection regime for children's homes was proposed. The programme also highlighted the need to improve care planning by strengthening the role of the Independent Reviewing Officer to ensure that the child's voice is heard when important decisions that affect his or her future are taken. In addition, the need to ensure that young people up to 18 are not forced out of care before they are ready by giving them a greater say over moves to independent living, and the need to provide more personal and financial support for care leavers are discussed. Other reforms, which have been incorporated into the Children and Young Persons Act 2008, included a new general duty on local authorities to take steps to ensure the availability of sufficient accommodation that is appropriate for the needs of the children and young people they look after within their local authority area, unless that is inconsistent with a child's welfare. In addition, unless it is inconsistent with a child's welfare, local authorities will have to give preference to placing a child with a relative, near their home, and with siblings, if they are also in care. They are also required to ensure that education or training is not disrupted, ensure that every school has a designated teacher for children in care which will promote and encourage their achievement, and ensure those who enter custody are visited regularly by the responsible local authority.

However, while such aspirations are again laudable, they have in practice proved difficult to implement. For example, given the reduction in local authority children's homes which has occurred over recent years, and reliance upon often out of area private provision, it is unlikely that within current budgetary constraints and cutbacks, councils will be able to fulfil the requirement to provide sufficient residential accommodation within their areas for those young people who need it. In addition, while local authorities might be encouraged to have higher aspirations for young people in care, financial restrictions will in all likelihood be a significant impediment to the realisation of this goal, along with the low expectations of some care-system workers and concomitant professional practice. Indeed, while Care Matters acknowledged that residential care has an important role to play as part of a range of placement options, the measures discussed do not address the culture, ethos and operation of children's homes, which have been found to be so productive of positive or negative outcomes (Whitaker, Archer and Hicks, 1998; Sinclair and Gibbs, 1998; Berridge and Brodie, 1998; Brown et al., 1998; Hicks et al., 2007; Anglin, 2002) and the variability in quality of placements. Nevertheless, the White Paper (p.57) does acknowledge that:

> It is therefore essential that the reforms focus on ensuring that the residential sector provides good quality care and that it is a valued and dynamic setting, able to support children in their development and enable them to move on where appropriate.

The need to improve the training of residential care staff was highlighted, along with the potential value of the popular European/Scandinavian model of residential child care, social pedagogy. A pilot programme to evaluate its effectiveness in the English residential care context was subsequently undertaken and led to some improvements in the perceptions of the young people about the quality of the care they received (ADCS, 2013). However, overall, there was a relative lack of measurable impact which the authors of the evaluation were forced to conclude is linked more broadly to social, political and cultural factors, pointing out that: 'social work in England (and the

USA) traditionally have an "individualist" approach compared with more collectivist or "reflexive-therapeutic" styles in other countries' (Berridge et al., 2011, p.256). It is undoubtedly the case that there is still a long way to go in terms of bringing English residential provision up to a consistently acceptable standard.

Developments since 2010

In 2010, a revised suite of regulations, guidance and National Minimum Standards for children's homes was published and came into effect in 2011, providing a new statutory framework for the residential child care sector (DfE, 2012b). Amongst other things, the revised framework emphasises the importance of the quality of children's relationships with residential staff and, in line with other recent guidance on services for children in care, includes an increased emphasis on care planning, giving an enhanced role to Independent Reviewing Officers. This involves the development of an individual placement plan, to facilitate the delegation of responsibility for day-to-day decisions and so support staff are able to take on a more 'normal' parental role. Also emphasised is the need to support staff and develop their skills in implementing a coherent behaviour management policy within each home (Berridge, Biehal and Henry, 2012).

Further efforts to improve the quality of children's residential care include the launch by the Coalition government in September 2010, of the Children's Homes Challenge and Improvement Programme. The aim of the programme has been to develop and share effective practice in the sector in order to improve standards of care. Part of its remit has been to improve knowledge of the way the residential sector is currently functioning and of the children and young people it serves, which has so far included analysis of existing data held by the DfE and Ofsted (resulting in the publication of the Children in Children's Homes in England Data Pack, DfE) and a short study commissioned by the Department for Education to provide a closer look at children's homes today and the views and characteristics of the children that they care for (Berridge, Biehal and Henry, 2012). Indeed, it has been highlighted how 'very little research on English residential care has been conducted since the mid-1990s, so new research is needed to assess the nature, use and outcomes of residential care in the current context' (ibid., p.7).

Developments in youth justice

When undertaking this study, it was further considered that the disadvantages experienced by young people in children's homes, as the result of both their pre-care experiences and the variable quality of care across the sector, might be compounded by developments in youth justice policy since the early 1990s and particularly since the election of the New Labour government in 1997, which have stressed the need for ever-earlier preventive formal intervention with children and young people thought to be at risk of offending or re-offending. Indeed, New Labour drew upon research which appeared to give credence to the view that particular 'risk factors' associated with a child's upbringing and family background had a profound effect on later behaviour and that if targeted at an early enough stage, problems could be 'nipped in the bud' (Soloman and Garside, 2008). Alongside this, there has been a rise in 'popular punitiveness' or authoritarianism in the wake of the media inflamed moral panic after the 1993 murder of James Bulger by two ten-year-old boys and the subsequent 'demonising' of child offenders. As a result of such factors, the two main political parties converged around a 'new correctionalism' (Muncie and Goldson, 2006), which 'eclipsed the traditional ideological differences that conventionally distinguished Conservative and Labour youth justice policies' (Goldson and Muncie, 2006, p.209). The emphasis came to rest upon young people and their families taking responsibility for their behaviour and indeed responsibility for change, thus 'individualising' the problem of crime:

> The youth justice system ... too often excuses the young offenders before it, implying that they cannot help their behaviour because of their social circumstances. Rarely are they confronted with their behaviour and helped to take responsibility for their actions. (Home Office, 1997)

In terms of criminological theory, the perception that crime fundamentally involves moral choice, which in turn is driven by failures in parental and self-control, is a key aspect of 'right realism'. Muncie (2000, p.17) explains how, over the years, various research has been cited in order to support this perspective, including that undertaken by Wilson and Herrrnstein (1985), who concluded that 'personality traits' such as impulsiveness and lack of regard for others are key factors in criminality, and that it is in 'discordant families' that such traits are to be found. It is stressed that criminality rests on *choice*: a choice mediated by the perceived costs and benefits of such action. Similarly, Gottfredson and Hirschi (1990) contend that the key factor underlying criminal behaviour is a lack of self-control, which in turn derives from factors affecting the calculation of one's acts and, most crucially, on effective socialisation. Muncie (2000, p.17) explains how this 'narrow interpretation of crime causation' came to dominate New Labour's criminal justice initiatives, despite evidence which suggests that situational, structural and socio-economic factors also have a part to play. Indeed, the perspective of 'left realism', associated with the work of John Lea and Jock Young (1984), although stressing that crime fundamentally involves moral choice, posits that a range of 'restricting circumstances' such as marginalisation and relative deprivation always mitigate that choice and certainly Goldson and Muncie (2006, p.222) highlight how:

> The children who are most heavily exposed to correctional intervention, surveillance and punishment within the youth justice system in England and Wales are routinely drawn from some of the most disadvantaged families, neighbourhoods and communities.

As children in care predominantly emanate from such circumstances, they consequently have the potential to be disproportionately affected by youth justice interventions. Nevertheless, seeking the political advantage in this area, New Labour embraced the idea of 'tough' responses to youth crime, thus emulating aspects of US policy and practice. Consequently, despite a reduction in youth crime figures (Nacro, 2009), the figures for youth incarceration (in terms of those both on remand and sentenced) rose (Pickford and Dugmore, 2012). Indeed, in contrast to 1993, when approximately 1,300 young people were detained, by January 2008 that figure had risen to just under 2,832 (Bateman, 2011; Pickford and Dugmore, 2012). This surge in numbers was out of step with other European Union countries and led the United Nations Committee on the Rights of the Child, in 2008, to register concern that this was indicative of a failure to ensure that detention was used as 'a matter of last resort', representing a breach of the United Nations Convention on the Rights of the Child (Bateman, 2011).

In contrast with earlier legislation such as the Children and Young Person's Act 1933, Section 44(1) and Section 1(1) of the Children Act 1989, which sought to prioritise the welfare of the child in court proceedings, the Crime and Disorder Act 1998 established the prevention of offending as the principal 'statutory aim' of the youth justice system (recently reiterated by the Criminal Justice and Immigration Act 2008). It also abolished the rebuttable presumption of doli incapax for those under the age of 14, thus firmly establishing the age of criminal responsibility in the UK as 10, one of the lowest in Western Europe. The Act entailed the ending of police discretion with regard to repeat cautioning, and the replacement of the caution with reprimands and final warnings which could only be imposed on a stipulated number of occasions before prosecution. The absolute and conditional discharge disposals previously imposed in 28 per cent of cases were replaced by the 1999 Youth Justice and Criminal Evidence Act with the Referral Order. In this way, more individuals were drawn into the youth justice system at an earlier point than might otherwise have been the case and indeed, between 1996 and 2006, the number of under-18s sentenced in court increased by 20 per cent (Prison Reform Trust 2008, p.4).

In addition, the numbers of first time entrants to the youth justice system increased exponentially to a peak of 110,815 in 2006–2007 (YJB/MoJ, 2012). Along with the ending of police discretion with regard to repeat cautioning and an almost trebling of out of court disposals (Pickford and Dugmore, 2012), it has been acknowledged that a significant contributory factor to this trend was the Offences Brought to Justice Target (OBTJ) which created targets for the police around the numbers of offences reported to them that should be brought to justice (i.e. resolved) and an offender given a pre-court disposal or conviction. Given the propensity of many children's homes to involve the police for minor incidents, such factors will undoubtedly have had a significant impact upon residents and indeed, for some time, there has been increasing disquiet from many sources concerning the desirability of such initiatives and their 'net widening' effects. Writing for *The Guardian* the former chair of the Youth Justice Board, Rod Morgan (2007) argued that in order to meet crime targets, the police were 'picking low-hanging fruit – the lowest of which comprises juvenile group behaviour in schools, residential homes and public spaces, offences that could be dealt with informally, more effectively, speedily and cheaply, and in former times were'. In point of fact, Pitts (2003, p.80) describes how:

> Earlier policies of diversion and minimalism were shaped by research evidence, which appeared to suggest that both punitive and rehabilitative programmes had a minimal impact upon re-offending (Martinson, 1974; Wilson, 1975) and that they sometimes worsened the problems that they were intended to solve, through the process of 'labelling'.

Certainly, McAra and McVie (2010, p.184) highlight how a key point of controversy with regard to 'early intervention' research is whether it is ever possible to predict with certainty which children will turn out to be serious offenders in their teenage and adult years, with some of the most robust studies (e.g. White et al., 1990) suggesting that there is likely to be a high false-positive rate. They also point out that moreover, a range of recent studies have focused on the longer term, damaging impact which system contact has on young people, with interventions being experienced as punitive and stigmatising and serving in the long term to amplify rather than diminish offending (e.g. Tracy and Kempf-Leonard, 1996; Huizinga et al., 2003; McAra and McVie, 2007). Reporting upon the Edinburgh Study of Youth Transitions and Crime, McAra and McVie (2010, pp.198–199) highlight how 'the deeper young people who were identified as the usual suspects penetrated the youth justice system, the less likely it was that their involvement in serious offending was inhibited' and that 'those who were brought to a hearing and placed on supervision were significantly more likely to be involved in serious offending one year later than their matched counterparts with no such hearings contact'. This is particularly galling when one considers that numerous self-report and other studies indicate that offending is a relatively 'normal' part of growing up for most young people, the majority of whom 'grow out of crime' (Rutherford, 1992; Goldson and Muncie, 2006, p.210).

In addition, as subsequent government initiatives have been selective in their choice of identified risk factors upon which they have chosen to focus with the preference being for personal, individual factors such as familial and developmental problems, as opposed to structural factors relating to offending such as government policy, unemployment, poverty, discrimination and marginalisation (Smith, 2007), it is clear that resultant interventions will only ever provide partial solutions.

Given that young people in care, particularly children's home residents, appear to have the potential to come to the attention of the youth justice system more often than might otherwise have been the case, it is clear that an emphasis upon formal early intervention (bringing with it a concomitant reduction in diversionary options) and an increasingly punitive emphasis on children taking responsibility for their actions, might have a disproportionately negative impact upon them. Indeed, Taylor (2006, pp.39–40) asserts that:

> New Labour's two pronged approach to protecting children and preventing criminality... has arguably resulted in a series of incoherent and contradictory policy assumptions that are particularly likely to impact upon young people in care. What are the implications of the current climate for young people in the care system, who may be in need of varying degrees of care and control?

Nevertheless, recent developments appear to provide grounds for cautious optimism. The number of first time entrants to the youth justice system has fallen by 59 per cent since 2001/2002, declining by 20 per cent from 45,910 in 2010/2011 to 36,677 in 2011/2012 (YJB, 2013). Undoubtedly, the primary reason for this can be found in the fact that the OBTJ target was replaced in April 2008 with one that placed more emphasis on bringing more serious crimes to justice and in December 2010 it was dropped entirely, bringing renewed discretion to frontline police ranks. The YJB (2013) states that it is also possible that diversionary work in the form of restorative justice and triage schemes undertaken by Youth Offending Teams and other partners have contributed to such reductions.

Similarly, there has since been a marked decline in the population of the secure estate for children and young people from 2008, with the figure for February 2013 being 1,320 (YJB, 2013). Allen (2011) concludes that rather than being the result of a deliberate or overt policy objective in central government, this unexpected fall, which represents the largest decline in custody for children since the 1980s, is a result of a number of interconnected factors. These include the aforementioned changes in the way that children are dealt with by the police, resulting in a consequent drop in overall numbers being sentenced by the courts, but also by a drop in the proportion sentenced to custody. Indeed, it is highlighted that despite dealing with smaller numbers of more serious and persistent cases, the courts have sentenced a lower percentage to custody which it is argued has been stimulated in part by changes in the law and sentencing guidance and in part by the improved performance and focus of YOT's, all encouraged by various campaign groups:

> There is some evidence of engagement between the Youth Justice Board and youth offending teams on the one hand and courts on the other which may have developed a shared view that custody should be a last resort. (ibid., p.4)

The Coalition government's Green Paper, *Breaking the Cycle* (MoJ, 2010, p.1), stresses that 'if we do not prevent and tackle offending by young people then the young offenders of today will become the prolific career criminals of tomorrow' and that 'intervening early in the lives of children at risk and their families, before behaviour becomes entrenched, can present our best chance to break the cycle of crime' (ibid., p.68). While there is again an emphasis upon targeting 'at risk' young people and their 'failing' families for intervention and support, the punitive rhetoric which accompanied New Labour's reforms is largely absent and instead, there is an acknowledgement that rigidly drawing young people into the youth justice system is not always either appropriate or necessary. It is stated that rather than a system out of court disposals where young people are automatically escalated to a more intensive intervention regardless of the circumstances or severity of their offence, 'an informal intervention could be more effective in making the young person face up to the consequences of their crime, provide reparation for victims and prevent further offending' (ibid., p.68). Certainly, the value of restorative justice is strongly endorsed and encouraged across the youth justice sentencing framework as a whole. A simplification of the legal framework to allow police and prosecutors greater discretion in dealing with youth crime before it reaches court was proposed, along with an end to the system of automatic escalation. Oversight

of Youth Offending Teams was henceforth to be centred on the three
key outcomes of: reducing the number of first time entrants to the
youth justice system, reducing reoffending and reducing custody
numbers. Indeed, the paper states that custody should be:

> Used sparingly as a last resort as it separates young people from
> their families and communities, can seriously disrupt education,
> training and development and is an expensive option that does
> not deliver good outcomes for young people. (ibid., p.70)

At the time this appeared to represent an encouraging acknowledgement of the potential harm wrought by imprisonment, including
high recidivism rates, and while undoubtedly in part financially
motivated by the costs associated with a rising custodial population,
rather than exclusively welfare related and/or ideological concerns,
was nevertheless seen by many as a welcome development.

Following on from this, the Legal Aid Sentencing and Punishment of
Offenders Act 2012 abolished the system of reprimands and warnings
that together were known as the Final Warning Scheme and introduced
Youth Cautions, a formal out of court disposal which, along with Youth
Conditional Cautions, can be used as an alternative to prosecution for
young offenders (aged 10–17) in certain circumstances. The significant point to note from this are that youth cautions are intended to
allow a more flexible response to offending: youth cautions and other
out of court disposals do not have to be used in a set order and are
available if a young person has been previously convicted. Similarly,
under Section 79 courts will now have more discretion to condition-
ally discharge a young person who pleads guilty to their first offence
instead of giving a Referral Order and the Act removes the current
restrictions and allows for repeated use of Referral Orders in line with
the commitment in the green paper to increase the use of restorative justice. Somewhat controversially, the Act now enables breach
proceedings to be brought even after a Detention and Training Order
(the term used to refer to a period of imprisonment and subsequent
licence supervision for those under 18) has finished, and punishment
for such a breach can include a period of imprisonment. However, a
stated aim of the Act is to reduce the use of secure remand for children
and young people and new provisions under Sections 90–107 of the
Act have been introduced to facilitate this.

In addition, the status of 'looked-after child' will apply to all young people on remand and the costs of keeping a young person in custody on remand will be transferred to local authorities, in order to provide an incentive to use this option more sparingly. Therefore overall there is a definite commitment to returning more discretion to the frontline youth justice professionals, albeit within closely defined parameters and an acknowledgement that formal intervention can be counterproductive. This, along with the other developments alluded to could well have a positive impact upon children and young people in residential care who have a greater likelihood of coming to official attention.

Nevertheless, given the often persistent nature of the challenging and troublesome behaviour exhibited by individuals in children's homes and the reliance by staff upon police intervention in many instances, it is likely that they will remain at a disadvantage when compared to other young people. For example, the guidance material (MoJ, 2013) relating to youth cautions makes it clear that a young person's offending history should be taken into consideration when deciding whether to administer such a disposal, stating that decision makers should consider whether the new offence is part of a pattern of offending that requires a more serious response such as a prosecution and that care must be taken to guard against 'inappropriate repeat cautioning' (ibid., p.10). This is particularly resonant for young people in residential provision, who, for a number of reasons relating to their experiences both prior to and subsequent to entering care might establish a 'pattern' of 'offending' which will result in their acceleration through the system to a point where custody becomes the inevitable outcome.

Indeed, Allen (2011, p.26) argues that along with introducing more rigorous statutory criteria for custody, 'raising the age at which children can be imprisoned or even prosecuted would cement the achievements of the last few years in reducing child imprisonment in line with the UK's obligations under the UN Convention on the Rights of the Child'. Certainly, while the UK retains its current low age of criminal responsibility, it is undoubtedly the case that children and young people in care will continue to be criminalised in a way which will adversely affect them throughout their lives. Dealing with challenging youthful behaviour via non-criminal routes, as is the case in other European countries, would appear to be the logical response. However, in a country where authoritarian ideals are never very far from responses to youth crime, it will remain to be seen whether the current willingness to embrace a less punitive and interventionist approach can be maintained. Indeed, in his exploration of the reduction in child imprisonment, Allen (2011) argues that there may be the need to defend the gains that have been made. It is stated that while the cuts that are currently being made to public services may help to strengthen the case for diversionary and cost-effective approaches (of which a sparing use of custody is an example), 'if they lead to heightened public, professional and media concern about crime and the role that children play, the current approach may come under pressure from those who favour a harsher response to children in trouble' (ibid., p.26).

Certainly, in what appears to be a direct departure from the anti-custodial rhetoric of the *Breaking the Cycle* Green Paper, the Justice Secretary, Chris Greyling indicated in February 2013 that incarcerating child offenders and ensuring rigorous education and training is the way to encourage young people 'to turn their backs on crime for good' (Winnett, 2013). The idea that young people should be sent to 'secure colleges' similar to modern-day borstals to be rehabilitated was met with dismay by those who consider that prison is not the place to educate young people. Indeed, Francis Crook, chief executive of the Howard League for Penal Reform argues that,

> Confusion is at the heart of these plans, which risk repeating the mistakes of history such as the failing secure training centres, where reoffending is sky-high and two children have died ... Almost all the children who end up in custody could be dealt with in the community and that is the way to get them back into school, college or training. (Winnett, 2013)

Nevertheless, at the time of writing, the Coalition Government appears to be intent on taking the plans forward with Mr Grayling stating in May 2013 that teachers should be encouraged to build detention centres next to existing specialist schools. This appears to represent a backward step in the progress that has been made to reduce numbers in custody and it will remain to be seen what the long-term impact of such measures, if implemented, will be, particularly for children and young people in residential care. In addition, it should again be borne in mind that although the punitive rhetoric may have largely disappeared, the focus of restorative justice interventions championed by the *Breaking the Cycle* Green Paper and subsequent legislation, are essentially focused upon the deficits of the identified young person with the onus being placed first and foremost upon individuals to accept responsibility for their actions, thus side-lining consideration of the wider contributory factors that are undoubtedly so pertinent to youth justice involvement, most notably for children's home residents.

Conclusion

In summary, it is evident that a number of policy and practice initiatives in both the care and youth justice contexts have the potential to impact in positive and negative ways upon the experiences and outcomes of children and young people in residential care. However, the long-standing contradictions that exist with regard to their position as vulnerable children in need of care and protection and their status as fully responsible offenders when they get into trouble is something that will not be easily resolved within a society where authoritarian and individualising discourses are so deeply embedded. Such factors will be further considered in the following chapter in connection with the theoretical underpinnings of the study; this will then be followed by a discussion of the studies' methodology.

3
Introducing the Research Study: Theory and Method

The research was underpinned by an eclectic range of theoretical perspectives which seek to explain human behaviour at the individual, institutional and systemic levels and the following chapter will explore these. After advancing the theoretical framework which informed the study, the chapter then moves on to outline the research strategy and methods adopted in relation to the empirical work upon which subsequent chapters are based.

Identity, reputation and power

When considering why young people in residential care might come to the attention of the youth justice system, it is first necessary to consider why they might begin to offend in the first place. As previously discussed, this could be linked to factors that pre-date the young person being received into care, factors which may continue to exert a powerful influence during their subsequent placements. As such, the work of Monica Barry (2006) around the search for 'social recognition' provides a useful platform from which to consider the triggers which might both precipitate offending and contribute to its continuance. When the young person enters a children's home, they then experience a further range of factors specific to residence in that particular environment which have the potential to influence behaviour in both positive and negative ways. Here, Goffman's (1961) interactionist perspective enables a valuable consideration of how and why the exercise of power in such contexts can impact upon residents' behaviour. In addition, Foucault's theories concerning the nature of power (1978, 1977) are of relevance to young people's experiences both in individual children's homes and the wider care system. Finally and following on from this, Jacques Donzelot (1979) provides potentially useful insights into the functioning of youth justice, particularly how it links to and enforces the 'normalizing' authority of other social agencies.

The search for 'social recognition'

Utilising the concept of capital developed by Pierre Bourdieu, Barry (2006, p.3) links the onset of offending to the need for *social recognition*, defined as, 'the attainment of a durable and legitimate combination of capital accumulation and expenditure during the transition into adulthood'. She argues that:

> Moving through the phases of transition from childhood, through youth to adulthood, can be an isolating and disempowering experience for young people, not least when they also lack political and economic power...Children and young people are thus inherently vulnerable because of their age and status and are, in effect, a minority group with the same potential for exploitation, discrimination, domination, disrespect and non-recognition by adults. (ibid., 2006, p.1)

Barry suggests that as a result of such factors, some young people might find solace in their peers in the transition to adulthood and resort to crime as a means of gaining a valued reputation with others of a similar age or status. Indeed, she argues that, 'offending can be used as a strategy, however temporary or misguided, to give them a valuable source of identity, status and recognition, in an otherwise potentially marginalizing period of their lives' (ibid., 2006, p.6).

Certainly, considering that young people who come into care have often experienced disempowerment in the form of abuse and/or neglect within the context of their families, it is very possible that they might find solace with their peer group and (perhaps also influenced by the cultures of the areas in which they live: see Nayak, 2003) become involved in criminal activity. Such outlooks and strategies may well become ingrained and difficult to overcome, even after a young person is removed from their immediate family, peer group and area. Indeed, it is reasonable to assume that the desire for social recognition continues when the young people are placed in residential care, and, as such, has the potential to influence behaviour in that context in both positive and negative ways. In her ethnographic study of group experiences in residential care, Emond (2003, p.326) found that 'young people regarded the resident group as an important force in their day-to-day lives, their view of themselves and of their social world... individual position and status were a key element of the organization of groups'. Here, mainly positive benefits of group interaction were observed, although previous research has highlighted the potentially malign aspects of peer relationships in residential care (Polsky, 1962; Stewart et al., 1994).

The interactionist perspective

McIntosh et al. (2011, p.177) point out that 'given the highly regulated and surveilled nature of many of the spaces within the residential care home, it is often viewed and experienced by staff and children as being an 'institution' in its operation and ethos': certainly, a further trigger which has been identified for challenging and disruptive behaviour is the institutionalised nature of some homes and associated rigid rules and regulations (Kilpatrick et al., 2008). The research therefore considered how Goffman's (1961) interactionist perspective may still be applicable to children's experiences of residential child care. His study of one psychiatric hospital, 'Asylums', examines how institutions work, and considers how and why the exercise of power in such contexts can impact upon residents' behaviour.

Goffman utilises the concept of the 'total institution', those institutions which encompass the three key aspects of our life: work, play and sleep. While most people undertake these activities in different settings, for residents of total institutions, all these activities take place in the same site and under the same form of authority. Goffman argues that these institutions are, 'forcing houses for changing persons; each is a natural experiment on what can be done to the self' (1961, p.22). It is asserted that from the moment a person enters such an institution, they are required to accede to its authority, which involves what is identified as a 'degradation ceremony'. This takes place at the moment of admission to the institution, when a resident/inmate arrives carrying with them the signs and symbols of their own unique identity – clothes, hairstyle, jewellery. In order that the resident can be integrated into the total institution they must be stripped of the signs of this identity. Residents/inmates then adopt a number of strategies in order to cope with the regime, along a continuum which ranges from taking on board the values of the institution, to blatant resistance. The institution, in turn, operates in accordance with a system of 'punishments and privilege' (ibid., p.53), whereby cooperativeness or lack thereof, is responded to accordingly in order to maintain its authority.

Of course, many contemporary residential children's homes do not now operate along the lines of a 'total institution', with schooling and leisure activities often (although not invariably) taking place 'off site' and with many units being much smaller than in previous years. Nevertheless, when young people arrive at a residential unit from their previous environments (whether that was their family home, foster care or another residential placement), although they may not be required to change their hairstyle or surrender jewellery, they are still required to 'fit in' and comply with the rules, regulations, expectations and ethos of the home. They may be required to get up at a particular time in the morning, eat meals at certain times, request permission to enter certain areas of the home (such as the kitchen) or to undertake activities that they would usually take for granted, attend school and comply with a curfew, all of which may be contrary to and conflict with, their prior experiences and consequent identities, values and sense of 'self'. Indeed, McIntosh et al. (2011) found that attempts to 'display family' within the institutional context often involved the use of mealtime practices, which were seen as essential to efforts to create a 'home' or a 'homely' ambiance within the units. It was 'often taken as a given by many staff that the creation of a family-like atmosphere was positive and had therapeutic benefits. The strong moral force and presence of the family and family home as an unquestionably "good thing" resonated strongly with many of the staff' (ibid., p.182).

Nevertheless, while welcomed by some, and having the potential to create a feeling of togetherness and belonging, this was a new experience for many young people in residential care, and some were ambivalent, resisting the notion of the residential unit being their home. At difficult times residents frequently resisted attending meals or 'subverted staff expectations in regard to table manners and behaviour' (ibid., p.188). Indeed, young people may adopt various tactics in order to cope with a regime which attempts to impose unfamiliar and/or rigid expectations in terms of conduct and attitude, however well meant, which might include resisting it via challenging behaviour. Given the highly surveilled nature of residential care and the acknowledged low threshold reported by some young people for police involvement, this, in turn, could lead to youth justice involvement.

Social institutions, disciplinary power and resistance

Michel Foucault's theories relating to disciplinary power in the context of social institutions are also of particular relevance. Frost, Mills and Stein (1999) discuss how, at the centre of Foucault's thought is the idea that social institutions are constructed as part of the exercise of power which governs even the most private aspects of our lives, they are the 'material expressions of the exercise of this power'. Foucault (1977) writes of the creation of an obedient subject, through the imposition of habits, rules and orders. In contrast to theories, such as those advocated under the umbrella of individual positivism, which place the human subject as the origin of meaning, the individual is viewed as, 'a container whose self-identity and psychological interior is largely a product of the relations of power, discourse and practice in which he or she is enmeshed' (Layder, 2006, p.126). In order to achieve disciplinary power in the context of social institutions such as the residential children's home, the techniques of hierarchical observation, normalizing judgement and examination, are utilised. Hierarchical observation constitutes a constant surveillance, the principle of which, although external in origin, eventually becomes internalised and self-regulating, while at the same time, 'there is pressure upon the individual to conform to some standard of "normality" whilst within the domain of surveillance' (Layder, 2006, p.122). The individual's own self-regulation is again absorbed as part of the general system of surveillance, which is exemplified by the use of dossiers, marking and classification systems (and other forms of appraisal and monitoring or examination). Disciplinary power is imposed not only at the level of the individual children's homes, but also by the external disciplinary (or social control) mechanisms of the wider care system with its rules, regulations and concomitant professional practices.

Certainly, life in contemporary children's homes is one of surveillance, with the activities of residents monitored through the keeping of copious records relating to their everyday movements and activities, as well as their overall progress. While resident in such placements they are required to act in accordance with prescribed standards of normality, which for a number of children and young people, may have positive benefits: for example, a 2009 Ofsted report (Morgan, 2009) found that some young people felt that staff making sure that they got up on time and being made to go to school or do homework, had helped them to do well with their education.

Nevertheless, Foucault (1978) also asserts that where there is power, there is resistance. Therefore, although certain official standards of 'normality' may be imposed within the domain of children's homes, which are in turn usually in accordance with the dominant discourses of wider society (relating, for example to conceptions of appropriate childhood behaviour, gender roles and so forth), young people within the homes may behave in ways which are consistent with previously imposed standards of normality, emanating from their family, peer group, or community. This is congruent with Foucault's assertion that, 'power is everywhere' (1978, p.122) and 'not simply the province of privileged or "legitimate" authorities' (Layder, 2006, p.130). Such previous standards of normality may conflict with the dominant values of the children's home (and society), thus precipitating 'deviant' or 'challenging' behaviour. Indeed, such a perspective offers a useful insight into how life in children's homes could potentially shape the responses of their residents and prove challenging for young people who are required to adjust to the requirements of (sometimes numerous) regimes.

Such ideas can be linked to the theories of Donzelot (1979, p.50), who has asserted that from the mid-nineteenth century onwards, 'the state governed through the family by containing its members within prescribed limits'. This was achieved by the work of social agencies (including those concerned with welfare, the school or the juvenile court) who devised and disseminated 'expert knowledges', which have 'penetrated deep into the everyday life of the urban working classes' (Muncie, 2004, p.211), continuously devising remedies for the 'aberrant'. In this way, a 'tutelary complex' to 'watch over' the young and their families was formed by psychologists, paediatricians, social workers, teachers and health visitors, the aim of which was to, 'govern society by delegating legitimacy to professionals empowered to nurture individuals into social citizenship' (ibid., p.211). In this way, professionals were given the authority to oversee and enforce certain behavioural 'norms'. As amply illustrated in the previous chapter, departures from such norms could then be legitimately monitored and regulated, not only through formal criminal/youth justice legislation, but also, 'through an ever expanding range of familial and social policy interventions' (ibid., p.211).

Certainly, the influence of 'expert knowledges' in regulating society and defining what is considered to be 'normal' behaviour, is something which is arguably of relevance to the young people's experiences throughout their lives. This includes the involvement of social services with their often troubled families prior to entering care, in their individual children's homes, and in their experiences of the over-arching care and youth justice systems. When describing the function of juvenile law, Donzelot (1979) argues that its central importance is due to the pivotal position it occupies between an agency that sanctions offences (the retributive justice of ordinary law) and a composite group of agencies that distribute norms:

> On the one hand it endows them with an authority, a coercive capacity necessary for them to function. On the other hand, it filters out the negative products of the work of normalization. (p.112)

It could be argued that nowhere can this be more clearly seen than by the residential homes' recourse to the police for minor transgressions or the use of formal youth justice interventions to deal with troubled and troublesome young people. Indeed, along with the theories of Goffman (1961) and Foucault (1977, 1978), Donzelot's work provides a useful insight into the power and control exerted by social institutions, and how this may impact upon the lived experiences of children and young people in residential care.

Research strategy, methods and analysis

Having concluded that the reasons why young people in residential care might come to the attention of the youth justice system could potentially link to a number of pre- and in-care factors at individual, institutional and systemic levels, it was then necessary to consider the most appropriate means by which the research project could explore such factors. As touched upon in the introduction, the research questions for this study were as follows:

- What are the factors at individual, institutional and systemic (over-arching policy and practice) levels which contribute to young people in residential children's homes coming to the attention of the youth justice system?
- To what degree are such factors pertinent to youth justice involvement?
- How do the attitudes, perceptions and subsequent actions of professionals contribute to the experiences of the young people and consequent criminalization?

It was anticipated that documentary data (court records; pre-sentence reports; social services case files; records of previous convictions) would supply some of the basic information that was required regarding the background, circumstances and experiences of the young people. However, as such records are written by professionals and in some cases contain only minimal data, it was unlikely that they would provide the requisite detail and insight particularly in relation to how the young people felt about their experiences. Similarly, although some of the reports and records might contain professional perspectives, they would be unlikely to convey the thought processes of the individual workers regarding the system within which they were required to function and the young people with whom they worked. It was therefore felt that the answers to the research questions would lie primarily in the first-hand accounts of young people who had come to the attention of the youth justice system whilst in residential care as well as the professionals who work with them in the care and youth justice systems. Overall, such a perspective is in accordance with the qualitative research approach which 'seeks to describe and analyse the culture and behaviour of humans and their groups from the point of view of those being studied' (Bryman, 1988, p.46).

Of course, whilst the dependability and credibility of interview data was increased by the available documentary sources, it is important to bear in mind that the information provided was based upon subjective accounts of events; memories of experiences can become clouded over time and in the case of the young people may be further complicated by their often traumatic nature and by the 'fragmented picture that they may have as a result of movement and change' (Taylor, 2006). Nevertheless, such an approach has previously yielded extremely insightful data (e.g. Schofield, 2003; Taylor, 2006) and was considered to be particularly important in the context of this research as a means of empowering both the young people and those who worked with them to become part of the solution, and not simply passive subjects of scrutiny.

The remainder of this chapter will present an account of the research design and methods used in this study. Primary considerations were a focus on the research questions and respect for participants. The challenge was therefore to utilise an approach which would yield the necessary information without being overly intrusive and onerous to the young people and professionals, in accordance with prescribed ethical standards. These considerations permeated the entire research process, including the gathering of data, and when reporting the findings.

A case-study approach

With the above in mind, it was decided to undertake a case-study of a particular local authority area, hereafter referred to as 'Coalton'. Yin states that:

> In general, case studies are the preferred strategy when 'how' or 'why' questions are being posed, when the investigator has little control over events, and when the focus is on a contemporary phenomenon within a real life context. (1994, p.1)

The aim of the case-study was to gather information in order to ascertain the multifarious factors which had contributed to the young people coming to the attention of the youth justice system and the responses of the professionals, over the period of the young people's lives up to and including their time in residential care. Yin describes how:

> The case study's unique strength is its ability to deal with a full variety of evidence-documents, artefacts, interviews, and observations... (ibid., p.8)

As such, it was considered that this approach would enable the exploration of court records and case-file records; semi-structured interviews with the identified young people and professionals and a focus group, with a view to gathering the relevant information. A case study would facilitate an in-depth and detailed piece of qualitative research, focusing upon a relatively small geographical area and selected participant samples.

Compared to some of the larger, neighbouring conurbations, Coalton itself was relatively small and, for an individual researcher with limited time and resources, presented a manageable population size. Indeed, it was felt that the advantages of such practical considerations would outweigh other factors, such as the lack of ethnic and socio-economic diversity. Nevertheless, although the population of Coalton was predominantly white and exhibited notable levels of socio-economic disadvantage, this too provided scope for an exploration of particular cultural relations. With regard to the issue of gaining access to the relevant people and information, this was certainly made easier in some respects. However, given the sensitive nature of the research, it was far from straightforward in others, as will be described at a later stage.

Phases of the research

Between Wednesday 28 May and Monday 9 June 2008, a survey was undertaken of Coalton Magistrates Court records, dating from Friday 1 June 2007 to Friday 30 May 2008, the primary aim of which was to identify potential research participants by discovering how many young people accommodated in residential children's homes in the Coalton area at the time their offences were committed, were sentenced during the 12-month period. Lists of the addresses of registered public and private children's homes in the Coalton area were obtained from the local authority and Ofsted, thus enabling identification of the young people. In total, 18 young people were identified who fit the criteria, aged between 12 and 18. Ten were accommodated in private children's homes, nine of whom had originated from outside the Coalton area and were therefore the responsibility of other local authorities. The remaining eight were resident in Coalton local authority homes and were the responsibility of Coalton social services.

After the individual young people were identified, biographical information was collected: this included their ages at the times they were sentenced, gender and ethnic origins. Further relevant data included the number of times each young person was sentenced within the 12-month period and, where available, information regarding whether they had previous convictions, the nature of the offences for which they were sentenced and whether the offences were committed at the residential unit (against staff, fellow residents, or residential unit property). The sentence handed down to the young person was recorded, and, if given a custodial sentence, the magistrates' reasons for imposing such a disposal.

Having identified potential research participants from the court records survey, the aim was then, utilising a non-probability, purposive sampling strategy, to obtain the consent of as many as possible, to take part in the next stages of the research. Given the size of Coalton and the number of residential children's homes within its boundaries, it was always going to be unlikely that the survey would yield a sufficiently large number of young people to warrant probability sampling. However, Denscombe (2003, p.16) argues that 'the advantage of purposive sampling is that it allows the researcher to home in on people or events which there are good grounds for believing will be critical for the research' and in light of this, it was decided that itwould be appropriate to attempt to recruit all of the identified young people, in order to gain the benefit of as many perspectives and experiences as possible. An equal number of male and female respondents were not expected, due to the fact that overall recorded offending rates show that males vastly outnumber females. However, while it was not a stated aim of the study to draw comparisons between males and females, given that in all likelihood, 'the responses of young men and women would be different due to varied expectations, pressures and stereotypes' (Taylor, 2006, p.242), it was hoped that the participation of some young women could be secured. Nevertheless, it should be acknowledged that focusing upon the experiences of a relatively small sample of young people who have offended whilst in residential care necessarily limits the conclusions that can be drawn: the residential care population is diverse and contains young people who do not get into trouble.

Recruiting research participants

Having identified a potential sample of young people, the next phase of the research involved recruiting participants for the study. Of the eighteen young people originally identified from the court records survey, six agreed to participate in the research. Consequently, the research sample was supplemented by the recruitment of a further six young men through the Coalton branch of a charitable organisation that provided leaving care support services for Coalton local authority: all had offended whilst resident in children's homes in the Coalton area. With regard to those young people identified via the court records survey, the relevant social services departments were contacted and permission was negotiated through their individual caseworkers to approach them to take part in the research. With regard to those who were identified via the charitable organisation, permission to approach the young people was negotiated through their individual leaving care workers.

A relatively small number of the professional participants were approached as a result of their associations with the sample of young people. However, many others were identified from the my personal knowledge gained from my previous employment in the youth justice sector, which in turn produced further participants via a 'snowballing' effect. A limitation of such an approach is that it excludes from participation professionals of whom the researcher and her contacts are unaware. Nevertheless, as previously described, purposive sampling can be legitimately utilised to identify participants who are perceived to have the requisite knowledge and experience.

Potential participants were provided with written information about the study beforehand using age-appropriate language, that set out the nature and purpose of the research (why it was being done), how it would be conducted (the methods used), what would happen to the findings, who might benefit from them, and why they had been approached to take part. In this way, their informed consent was obtained to both undertake the interview and access relevant records relating to histories, care and youth justice experiences. In the case of the younger participants, the consent of whoever held parental authority was also obtained. Confidentiality was ensured by assigning pseudonyms from the outset to all of the young people and any geographical areas referred to, along with the secure storage of collected data. The

Table 3.1   Interview participants: children and young people

	Young person	Age	Location of interview
1	Emma	15	Children's home
2	Tom	15	YOI
3	Robbie	16	YOI
4	James	16	YOI
5	Lucy	17	Charity Office
6	Sarah	18	Home address
7	Daniel	18	Charity Office
8	David	18	YOT Office
9	John	18	Home address
10	Peter	20	YOI
11	Mark	20	YOI
12	Jack	22	Charity Office

Notes: 1–6 Children and young people identified from youth court records survey.
6–12 Young people identified via Charitable Organization, providing care and support for looked after children).
YOI = Young Offender's Institution
YOT = Youth Offending Team

professionals are referred to by their job title. Approval was obtained from the relevant University Ethics Committee.

In total 12 young people agreed to take part in the research, aged between 15 and 22 (see Table 3.1). Ten of the twelve participants were 'adolescent entrants' to the care system. There were three females and nine males – a gender imbalance which was in part precipitated by the more protective attitude of key workers towards their female service-users. Similarly, although younger children were identified in the survey of youth court records (the youngest was 11), key workers were reluctant to approach them, citing their vulnerability. The issue of adults' involvement in preventing looked after children from participating in research and the effect this has upon the number of children researchers are able to contact has been highlighted previously (Heptinstall, 2000) and it was clear from the outset that gaining the support and co-operation of case-workers and other more senior staff would be essential to facilitating access to the young people. Indeed, Masson (2000, p.36) points out that:

> Children and young people are rarely free to decide entirely for themselves whether or not to participate in research. The enclosed

nature of children's lives...means that they are surrounded by adults who can take on the role of 'gatekeepers', controlling researchers' access and children and young people's opportunities to express their views.

Although the study generally met with positive reactions, 'gatekeepers' were not always supportive, and occasionally denied access for arguably questionable reasons. For example, a case-worker felt that a particular 16 year old would agree to participate, but declined to approach her because she felt that taking part in the research would give her the message that if she behaved badly, she would receive attention: a somewhat over-zealous interpretation of behaviourist theory. Another felt that being approached to take part would convey to the young person that he was seen as an 'offender'. Masson (2000, p.36) argues that:

> Researchers should expect gatekeepers to try to protect children and young people from ill-conceived, valueless or potentially damaging research... However, gatekeepers can also use their position to censor children and young people.

Indeed, although it is to be expected that gatekeepers will be protective of young people's interests (and rightly so), this should not extend to denying them without consultation the opportunity to take part in research which could potentially prove both useful and empowering. This runs counter to the spirit of both domestic legislation and international convention which gives young people the right to be consulted before decisions are made about them commensurate with their levels of maturity and understanding. It also calls into question professionals' motives in doing so and certainly, Lee (1993) has argued that investigations are likely to have major implications for the researched and researchers alike when they meet one of three criteria: if they deal with private and stressful issues; when they study deviancy or social control; and where the emerging data might be stigmatising or incriminating in some way. It could be argued that this research had the potential to meet all three criteria, which might in part explain their reluctance; indeed, the question of whether such denials are in part motivated by the desire not to have their practice with young people subjected to scrutiny is a cause for concern. A small number of young people declined to participate after being approached for a variety of reasons.

With regard to the professional participants, the key-workers of the six young people identified by the court records survey agreed to be interviewed. These comprised of four field social workers (including the current and previous social worker of one young person), two Youth Offending Team (YOT) officers, and a Leaving Care worker. In addition, a further selection of professionals agreed to participate. These included four further YOT officers, two police officers, two Leaving Care workers and three residential children's home managers (two from the private sector units based in Coalton, and one from a voluntary Project in a neighbouring city), six magistrates, four legal advisers and four solicitors. Fourteen females and eighteen males were interviewed, the majority of whom were experienced practitioners in their fields. It is acknowledged that their perceptions may therefore differ from those at the beginning of their careers. Similarly, the police officers I was able to access worked for a Youth Offending Team and a Missing Persons Unit, the culture and outlook of which might be very different to general front-line police ranks.

A number of professionals were approached directly through their relevant agencies, organisations and firms, with a generally high degree of success. A notable exception to this was found in the reluctance of managers from both the public and private sectors, to allow their front-line residential care staff to be approached for interview, perhaps again relating in part to the sensitive and potentially incriminating nature of the research (Lee, 1993). However, eight residential workers from a children's home in a neighbouring city agreed to participate in a focus group and some of the other professionals, who had previously worked in public and private residential children's homes in Coalton, were able to recall their experiences.

Semi-structured interviews with young people and professionals

As illustrated by Table 3.1, the interviews with the young people took place at a variety of locations ranging from their homes (either children's homes or their own homes in the case of two of the older participants), social services offices and Young Offender Institutions. They were provided with the opportunity to ask questions about the research beforehand and assured that they could decline to answer any questions that they were not comfortable with and withdraw from the study at any time. Given that the young people were being asked to recall incidents which were potentially upsetting, they were offered the opportunity to engage with a counselling service after the interviews if they felt the need. In addition, the use of semi-structured interviews meant that the researcher had the flexibility to steer the conversation away from areas which were causing obvious discomfort. Indeed, the British Society of Criminology's code of ethical practice (2006) outlines how researchers should consider carefully the possibility that the research experience may be a disturbing one, particularly for those who are vulnerable by virtue of factors such as age, social status, or powerlessness and should seek to minimise such disturbances. It was made clear to the young people from the outset that while the research necessitated discussion of previous, mostly adjudicated offending, any information disclosed which indicated a potential risk of serious harm to either themselves or others, would be reported to the relevant authorities.

While remaining open to new insights, the possible explanations and areas for exploration generated by previous research were used as 'sensitizing concepts', providing a 'general sense of reference and guidance' (Blumer, 1954, p.7) during the data collection stages. Consequently, the young people were questioned about their pre-care experiences, including their family life and, where applicable, getting into trouble and contact with the youth justice system. Questions regarding in-care experiences centred primarily on relationships with other residents, staff members and key-workers, the residential regime and responses to challenging behaviour.

All of the professionals' interviews were conducted at the interviewee's place of work and at a mutually convenient time. Here, the focus was primarily upon perceptions of why young people get into trouble while in residential care, perceptions of the effectiveness or otherwise of residential homes and staff, how they responded to the young people when they got into trouble and the reasons for this and perceptions of the utility/effectiveness of the care and youth justice systems. Given their different professional backgrounds, it was inevitable that some of the interviewees would have more knowledge of certain subject areas than others, and the interviews were therefore modified accordingly.

In line with the qualitative approach outlined earlier, it was considered that such interviews would facilitate the confirmation of existing hypotheses, while potentially generating new insights into the reasons for the behaviour of the young people and professionals, based upon their individual perceptions and experiences. Certainly, latitude was given for deviation from pre-determined themes and questions were 'open'. Taylor (2006, p.70) argues that, 'such an approach places importance on the narrative provided by the inter-viewees, allowing them more freedom and control to articulate their experiences'.

With the exception of one of the young people, interviews were recorded. In the case of the young person who did not wish to be recorded, contemporaneous notes were made of the interview. The interviews varied in length, depending upon the amount that each individual participant had to say, and external considerations and constraints, including time limits in custodial institutions. The shortest interview lasted approximately 20 minutes, and the longest around an hour and a half.

As previously explained, in addition to the interviews, eight resi-dential care staff from a children's home operated by a charitable organisation in a neighbouring city (a mixture of men and women) agreed to participate in a focus group. The focus group lasted for approximately 45 minutes and with the participants' permission, it was recorded. Discussion primarily centred upon perceptions of why young people get into trouble while in residential care, how they responded to the young people when they got into trouble and the reasons for this and perceptions of utility/effectiveness of the care and youth justice systems. Although a disadvantage of group discussions are that less confident people might feel inhibited from putting forward their views, attempts were made to minimise such obstacles by asking if there were any other opinions and responding in a positive and encouraging way when people spoke. All of the people who agreed to take part contributed to the discussion to a greater or lesser extent and indeed, Morgan (1988, p.18) argues that, 'participants' interaction among themselves replaces their interac-tion with the interviewer, leading to a greater emphasis on partici-pants' points of view'. This was certainly the case in respect of this particular group of respondents; they debated various points with each other, sometimes forming a group consensus, while at other times proffering different points of view. This exercise yielded some rich and insightful data. Of course, it should be acknowledged that staff working in a home operated by a charitable organisation might have a different ethos, experiences and outlook to those working in the public or private sector, which would influence the nature of the data collected.

Data processing, analysis and verification

The next part of the research involved the various stages of processing and analysing the collected data (Straus and Corbin, 1988). With regard to the issue of the generalisability of the case study research, Yin (1994) makes the point that this involves aiming towards analytic (rather than statistical) generalisation and similarly, Pawson and Tilley (1997) suggest that it is sets of ideas and theoretical notions that are transferrable between cases, not lumps of data. According to Mitchell:

> The extent to which generalisation may be made from case studies depends upon the adequacy of the underlying theory and the whole corpus of related knowledge of which the case is analysed rather than the particular instance itself. (1983, p.203)

Therefore, the data was analysed with reference to the theoretical perspectives described in the first half of this chapter as well as qualitative findings from a wide range of other empirical studies.

I personally transcribed the recordings of the interviews and focus group in order to familiarise myself with the data and get an over-all feel for the content. The transcripts were then read and reread in order to enhance the process of familiarisation. From this it was possible to identify the themes that were common across the interviews. As alluded to previously, there were two kinds of themes: those that were inevitably there as a result of the topics covered in the interviews, and those that could be identified as being additional to these, arising from the way in which respondents had answered the questions.

All the themes identified in the interviews, focus group and documentary data were then integrated into a coding structure. Once this had been done it was possible to work with the coded data to develop ideas about how the themes linked together, and then to integrate them into thematic categories. This led on to interpreting the major themes: discerning patterns of meaning and explanatory concepts and developing statements of relationships between influences, case incidents or patterns, and consequences.

Overall, it was considered that the use of multiple sources of evidence – 'methodological triangulation' – would facilitate the in-depth exploration of the research questions, providing a different angle and perspective on the same course of events. This would also help to guard against deficits in the memories of interviewees, and potential information inaccuracies, thus increasing the credibility and dependability of the project. With regard to the information contained within the documentary data (Pre-Sentence Reports, court records and case-file information) it was useful to bear in mind the potential pitfalls of such secondary data, including possible inaccuracies in the information recorded, and the fact that conclusions reached, for example regarding reasons for offending behaviour and how it should be dealt with, would invariably be influenced by dominant professional discourse. However, consideration of such discourse as a separate theme, in itself provided useful insights into how and why professionals respond when the young people get into trouble.

Conclusion

This chapter began by introducing the eclectic range of theoretical perspectives used to inform the research, focusing particularly on the themes of 'identity, reputation and power' at the individual, institutional and wider systemic levels. It was argued that such perspectives offer a valuable means of illuminating the actions of the both young people and professionals, as they relate to youth justice involvement. Following the theoretical discussion, there was an exploration of the methodological approach adopted for this study, which involved using primarily qualitative methods to gain insights into why the young people might get into trouble. The subsequent chapters detail, discuss and analyse the findings which emerged from the research participants and other data sources.

Part II
Research Findings

4
Disempowerment, Responsibility and Difference

Introduction

As expected, given previous research (Sinclair and Gibbs, 1998; Darker, Ward and Caulfield, 2008), all except two of the young people interviewed had experienced some degree of contact with the youth justice system prior to entering residential children's homes. This ranged from being made the subject of low-level pre-court disposals such as a Youth Caution, to being sentenced to a period of imprisonment. This chapter will begin by exploring the young people's their accounts of how and why they began to get into trouble and the implications that this has for future offending in the residential care context. Their beliefs regarding the reasons that they were taken into care will also be highlighted, with consideration given to how this might impact upon subsequent self-perception and behaviour.

After the perceptions of the young people have been highlighted and analysed, the chapter will then proceed to incorporate a discussion of the 'individualisation' of offending and troublesome behaviour by the social workers who took part in the research. Indeed, while family background and pre-care experiences were viewed as being a strong contributory factor to the young people's psychological make-up and consequent actions amongst all the professional groups, it was also noticeable how an initial sympathy for their situation began to change into a focus upon individual responsibility. The implications of such attitudes upon responses to young people who get into trouble while in residential care will be considered.

Onset of offending: the need for social recognition?

In accordance with Barry's (2006) hypothesis regarding young people's need for social recognition, many participants stated that they began to get into trouble out of a desire to fit in with a particular peer group:

> Being naughty with me mates, you know…Just shoplifting and stuff, going out, not going to school. (David, 18)

For some of the young people, drinking alcohol and using illegal drugs seemed to be an important part of peer group membership, and their resultant identity at that time; consequently, some offended in order to obtain money to buy these substances, or offended whilst under their influence:

> I eventually just got to the point where I started stealing for drugs…When I started smoking weed it were all peer pressure. I didn't want to do it, but everyone else were doing it, they were putting it in my face, so I just took it. (John, 18)
>
> I think really, if I'd stayed being good, not drinking, I don't think my life would be like this now. I don't know. I think it would be different. I think drugs and alcohol set me off on a different way of teenage life. (Lucy, 17)

Bromley (1993, p.33) argues that disempowered individuals and groups are likely to focus on their immediate group for the development of identity and reputation: 'membership of a minority group of like-minded individuals can be an effective buffer against a hostile majority'. Certainly, the young people in this study experienced disempowerment as the result of a number of factors which is illustrated by Lucy, who describes how she started getting into trouble as the result of a desire to get even with her mother for failing to protect her when she was younger:

> She'd hurt me when I were younger, right. I thought, at eleven, that drinking might help me, so I started drinking with me mates, getting drunk, taking drugs and stuff, and when me mam were telling me no, I kept doing it even more, because she had hurt me, so I were hurting her in a different way. (Lucy, 17)

Violence and neglect at the hands of a male parental figure was a theme that emerged in many of the interviews:

> I was 12 or 13 when I first went to Court for theft out of car, or doing credit cards... Dad let me do what I wanted, cos he was on heroin... Got up to all sorts... I ran away cos he used to take it out on me, give us a hiding. (Peter, 20)

> I never got along with my step-dad. I think that's why it all started in the first place... I used to argue with my dad and go out and get into trouble, then my dad used to hit me... I stabbed him because he were beating my mum up and pushing her around. (John, 18)

It is argued by Matza that powerlessness is a key factor in producing drift, and therefore delinquency: 'Being pushed around puts the delinquent in a mood of fatalism... In that condition he is rendered irresponsible' (Matza, 1964, p.89). John's disempowerment at that time emanated from his status as a child, in both physical and social terms and resulted in him being vulnerable to the actions of his step-father, about which he could do relatively little, other than seek to escape and find solace with his offending peer group. Indeed, it has been suggested that young people move from a feeling of disempowerment and worthlessness within the family to a feeling of confidence and well-being within the peer group (Ungar, 2000), which, for John and a number of the other interviewees, was undoubtedly the case. Certainly, when the young people were later removed from their families, peer group association again provided a means of empowerment in a situation where they were not otherwise in control. Indeed, this is a state of affairs which is discussed in much greater detail in the following chapter, particularly in relation to instances of solidarity with other residents. While for many, this may produce positive effects (Emond, 2003), for others it was a reason why offending behaviour often continued or even increased, despite them being removed from their families and to different settings:

> I kept getting moved just to get away from people, but everywhere I went, because of my reputation, I could just get on with anyone. I could just go out there and blend in like that with anyone. As long as they were bad though. It was always the bad people. I could never get on with the good people. (John, 18)

Waiton (2001) suggests that:

> Young people develop their own friendships based not on offending per se, but on equality, intimacy and mutual understanding; positive factors which for many young people tend not to be present in their relationships with adults.

Indeed, at various times, both when living with his family, and in subsequent care placements, John appears to have identified with, and been drawn to, other 'bad' young people, who he felt were on his wavelength. After experiencing an abusive family background and in the absence of 'legitimate' achievements, he seems to have gained a degree of personal pride and satisfaction from his ability to form these friendships and associations. John's consequent negative self-image meant that he was drawn to others he felt he could relate to. These friendships and associations, however fleeting or transitory, undoubtedly gave him some sense of self worth, possibly because they were not judgemental of, or critical towards him, in the way that family members, and professionals within the care and youth justice systems, certainly were. Nevertheless, in accordance with the idea that individual power and status increases in adulthood, John later describes how he feels that the balance of power has moved in his favour, now that both he and his step-father, are older:

> Right now, he's scared of me...Then, I couldn't do anything, cos he was younger...When I was 12, he was about 33, so he was bigger than me, well bigger than me. But not anymore. He's old, he's got grey hair, and he knows that if he grabbed me now...I couldn't be held responsible...I'd kill him. And he knows that. So now, he's not as cheeky with me anymore. (John, 18)

Indeed, the notion of rejecting dominant conceptions of childhood and its inherent powerlessness in favour of an accelerated transition to adulthood was something alluded to by a number of participants when they described growing up 'too quickly':

> I got chucked out in year seven. Just hanging about with the wrong people again, really. Put me in them little Exclusion Unit things. I don't really know. It's like I grew up too quick, know what I mean? (Robbie, 17)

When describing the experiences of the socio-economically disadvantaged 'Charver Kids' she had studied in the context of her research, Nayak (2003, p.89) reports how their experiences were, 'located outside the youthscapes of most working and middle-class childhoods' and that they 'blurred the boundaries between childhood and adult status'. Certainly, along with the illicit drug and alcohol consumption already discussed, many of the interviewees described neglected childhoods in which they appear to have participated in activities and been afforded freedoms, including staying away from the parental home for long periods, which one would normally associate with older people. Many had been excluded from or decided not to attend school, and rejected the value of educational achievement as a legitimate goal, thus providing further opportunities to get into trouble:

> They said I'd get good GCSE's (qualifications). But I weren't bothered. Was never interested in school. Just going behind the sheds for a smoke. (David, 18)
>
> Didn't go to school from age 12–13, me dad let me stay off ... Couldn't keep out of trouble. (Peter, 20)
>
> I wouldn't say I was dumb – I can read and write...but education and that don't really bother me. I learned everything I needed to learn in primary school. (Robbie, 17)

Given the often turbulent family experiences and social circumstances of many of the young participants, it is little wonder that educational achievement might have been low on their list of priorities. Indeed, Francis (2008, p.21) highlights how 'many young people come into public care with a history of educational difficulties' which 'usually stem from their experience of social exclusion and multiple disadvantage' (Brodie, 2001; Francis, Thomson and Mills, 1996; Packman and Hall, 1998). Nevertheless, there may also have been an element of machismo in the pronouncements of the young men based upon their working class cultural heritage. Indeed, Cassen and Kingdon (2007) found that white working class boys perform worse than any other ethnic or gender group at school. They claim that this is because a culture exists in their communities whereby it is seen as 'uncool' to learn, and that reading is seen as a 'feminine' or an 'unmanly' thing to do. However, it is also of note that amongst the young women interviewed, a similar disregard of the academic value of school emerged, suggesting that the influence of such cultural values can extend to both genders:

> I loved going to school...It weren't for me to learn, it were more like for me to see me friends and have a social life! (Lucy, 17)

Research recently published by the Equality and Human Rights Commission (2009) revealed that gender attitudes in schools have not changed since the 1960s and that within education and careers services, the expectations for white, working class girls are relatively low. It was found that for almost half of the girls interviewed from a working class background, a profound fear of failure was seriously affecting their chances at school and work. Therefore, it is apparent that both class and gender have the potential to significantly impact upon educational engagement and performance, albeit in different ways for males and females. Furthermore, Francis (2008) reports that entering care does not necessarily ameliorate the effects of earlier disengagement and low expectations, with research revealing that factors including placement instability, and the low expectations of professionals, adversely affects educational progress. Indeed, the potential for professional attitudes and systemic deficiencies to further compound existing difficulties for young people received into care are themes which unfortunately will be revisited on numerous occasions throughout this book.

The effect of prior experiences

Many of the young people described committing offences both within the residential homes and outside in the community, as the result of feelings of anger and frustration regarding what had happened to them prior to being received into care:

> Things went through me head, and it just clicks, and I go mad. And that's what it was both times, me anger, it just goes overboard. Cos I hold that much stuff inside me and don't speak to anyone about my life. (Lucy, 17)

Taylor (2006, p.90) refers to the concept of 'letting off steam' which relates to serious past trauma affecting current behaviour as the impact of their previous experiences begins to hit young people, and they get into trouble. As discussed, many of the young people in this research experienced tumultuous family backgrounds, some specifically being the subject of abuse and/or neglect. In addition to this, they were often rejected by their families, which will have had a profound impact upon their feelings of self-esteem and worth. Indeed, as will be discussed further in due course, the fact that many of the children and young people blamed themselves for their situation is testament to that. It is therefore little wonder that they might become angry and lash out at times when those feelings became too much, or, as in the case of John, turn that anger and frustration back upon themselves:

> Anger...I used to punch doors and break plates...I just trashed a care home. I smashed all the cups all over the place, tables; chairs. But then, because I kept getting done for that, I just started self-harming instead. Instead of getting arrested for all them stupid things, I just started cutting myself. It just takes your mind off summat. You just focus on the pain on your arm. (John, 18)

Similarly, when asked why he felt that he continued to get into trouble, Robbie replied:

> Everything gets me angry. I think it's the fact that I was put away in care at a young age, and I didn't understand why, and no-one was explaining to me why I got took into care. Mum and dad split up and obviously, I weren't in my home, and I went into a care home. I never spoke about it until a couple of years ago, kept it all in. It just got me angry. Just kept building up, and when I thought about it, it came out worse. (Robbie, 17)

Research evidence suggests high levels of emotional and behavioural problems amongst young people entering residential children's homes (Berridge and Brodie 1998) and Van Bienum (2008) reports how research has found a high prevalence of mental health disorders in children and young people in care. A study undertaken by McCann et al. (1996) is highlighted, which found a point prevalence rate of 67 per cent for psychiatric disorders in teenagers living in residential units and foster care, compared with 15 per cent of adolescents who lived with their own families. In addition, Meltzer et al. (2004) found that 49 per cent of eleven- to fifteen-year-olds in care had a psychiatric disorder sufficiently severe to impair their social functioning, compared to 11 per cent of children living in private households. The most common mental health problems were found to be conduct disorders (around 40 per cent, compared to 5 per cent in children in private households), followed by emotional disorders (12 per cent compared with 6 per cent). In terms of placement type, the highest rates (68 per cent) of mental disorder were found in those who were looked after and accommodated in residential homes. Given that the narratives of many of the young people in this study highlight abusive and/or neglectful pre-care experiences, it is unsurprising that they might exhibit challenging behaviour when placed in children's homes and consequently require working with in ways which recognise and attempt to negate the impact of such experiences. The following chapter will highlight ways of working which have been found to produce positive results with young people in residential care settings.

Community disempowerment

Disempowerment can occur not just at an individual level, such as through experiences with immediate family or at school, but also, more generally, at a community level. Although the young people did not all originate from the same area, they came from northern, post-industrial communities that had been affected by the cessation of previously thriving manual industries, precipitating subsequent unemployment and relative poverty. Nayak (2003) highlights how living in such communities can contribute to the perpetuation of illegal activity as a means of contributing to the household economy; indeed, some of the interviewees spoke of offending at various times in their lives, as a means of obtaining extra money to supplement a meagre income. Others alluded to experiences of family criminality by parents and step-parents, older siblings, aunts and uncles:

> He used to have flash cars and stuff, and I thought he was working and that, but obviously it must have been through all the drug money. I thought he was the big geezer and that. (David, 18)

Experiences of parental drug misuse and consequent police involvement in their lives when they were growing up were also mentioned. Brothers Daniel and Jack both spoke of their mum using drugs when they were younger, and of their dad having continued to use drugs over many years, along with intermittent periods of imprisonment. Both boys later went on to use 'soft' drugs and get into trouble. Peter's dad became addicted to heroin, and, as previously described, he spoke of this directly influencing his own offending. These young people lived in communities where drugs were readily available and police involvement in their lives from a young age appeared to be the norm. It is therefore unsurprising that some may have come to view involvement with the youth justice system with a degree of complaisance and a sense of inevitability.

Overall therefore, it is clear that the young people in this study experienced multiple pre-care disadvantages which adversely affected their subsequent behaviour. Certainly, as a consequence of the culmination of the factors discussed thus far, the young people were more likely to get into trouble than might otherwise have been the case and in fact Barry argues that:

> For many children from disadvantaged communities, 'childhood' does not offer the same type of protection that it offers young people from more affluent communities...thus questioning the traditional image of childhood as being a time of innocence and protection. (2006, p.27)

For many of the young people in this study, innocence and protection were not characteristics of their childhoods; rather neglect, violence and family discord predominated, compounded still further by socio-economic disadvantage and consequent disengagement with school. Under such circumstances, it is little wonder that relinquishing their childhood status and its attendant vulnerability might be seen as desirable by some. However, from an adult perspective, the development of such 'un-child-like' characteristics can often be perceived as 'unnatural' or threatening. This was something which undoubtedly impacted upon professional responses and is a theme which will be returned to at various points.

Self-blame

It was of note that whilst neglect, domestic violence, abuse and community disadvantage were frequently alluded to as being integral to their pre-care experiences, the majority of the young people attributed their inception into care as primarily being the result of their own behaviour. Indeed, although they were able to identify how other factors might have played a part, a sense of personal responsibility for the things that had happened to them both prior and subsequent to their time in care was a prevalent theme amongst nearly all those interviewed. This is exemplified by John's account, as despite being a victim of domestic violence at the hands of his step-father, he describes feeling how it was *his* subsequent behaviour that caused problems within his family:

> Now they all get on because I've started behaving. So I split the family up altogether. (John, 18)

When detailing the effects of powerlessness in relationships, Layder (2004, p.95) describes how, if a person is, 'dominated, put down or abused by another', this can lead to feelings of 'worthlessness and self blame'. Given the accounts of many of the young people, it is therefore unsurprising that they might experience these emotions. As previously discussed, John goes on to describe how this negative self image resulted in further offending, as he was subsequently drawn to other 'bad' young people who he felt were the same as him. It stands to reason that such feelings and emotions might not be very far below the surface for many of the young people and have the potential to profoundly impact upon their self-esteem, outlook; behaviour and expectations.

In addition, it became clear that such feelings have the potential to be further perpetuated by the attitudes and responses of professionals within the care and youth justice systems who in turn are predominantly influenced by the discourse of individual responsibility, to the exclusion of other factors. Certainly, as will be discussed in the following section, while the social workers and many other professionals interviewed as part of this research acknowledged the initial contribution of familial and social experiences to challenging and offending behaviour, their perceptions strongly reflected the idea these should not be used as an 'excuse' and that responsibility for change ultimately lay with the individual young people.

Individualisation: professional perceptions of responsibility

> His behaviour in Coalton was just the same as it were when he lived (at home). He was still drawn to certain friends and people, he was still drawn to the same situations... He seems to still be drawn to the same pattern of behaviour, no matter where he's living. (Social Worker)

As illustrated by the above quote, and in accordance with the accounts of the young people, the social workers felt that offending behaviour was often a continuation of what had been happening in the home environment. Nevertheless, there was little or no acknowledgement of the contribution of socio-economic factors or the specific community contexts from which the young people emanated; somewhat predictably the discourse of 'failing families' predominated. Indeed, the emphasis placed upon *pre-care* experiences being an explanation for *in-care* offending by the social workers, was in line with an overall perception on the part of many of the other professionals, that in-care offending was predominantly the result of individual psycho-social deficits, precipitated by family background:

> I think with children in care, it sort of depends upon what their initial background has been. If they've been taken away from their parents because their parents have been involved in criminal activity and drugs, and they sort of grow up in that environment... I think... it's like a natural progression for them to follow on the sort the lifestyle that their parents have led. (Police Officer)

Nevertheless, although family background was viewed as being a strong contributory factor to the young people's psychological make-up and consequent actions, it was also noticeable how it was often felt that individual choice still had a part to play:

> It's strange though, because James' sister, I'm the worker for his sister as well; she's totally different. She hasn't got into trouble, no offending. Although she's... younger than him, she's so much more mature in a lot of ways. She's a pleasure, she really is... She's come from the same background, but must just have handled it differently. (Social Worker)

Here, James' social worker clearly felt that despite his troubled background, he could have made different choices and stayed out of trouble had he wished, like his younger sister. Indeed, amongst the social workers, troublesome behaviour was often seen as a conscious choice on the part of the young people, utilised as a means to an end:

> I mean, they're not all young offenders. Some are brilliant. It's down to the individual. People make choices at the end of the day... I just think that they learn from what they're doing. They know that they can control the situation to some degree. And if they don't like something, they know that if they kick off, it will eventually change, and they'll be put somewhere else... They know if they do X, Y or Z, that's going to get a result... They learn to manipulate things. (Social Worker)

Smith (2009b) argues that externally imposed definitions tend to view children as one-dimensional, in that they are seen as either passive or active, but not both. He highlights earlier work by Packman, Randall and Jacques (1986), who demonstrate that responses to young people in the care system depend to an extent on whether they are typified as victims or villains. Indeed, in the context of this research, although the social workers initially viewed the young people as 'victims' of their family circumstances, this attitude changed when they continued to get into trouble while in care. In this context, they were viewed as active agents, responsible for their own actions, and, to a large extent, the author of their own misfortunes, having failed to avail themselves of the help on offer and recognise that the professionals had their 'best interests at heart'. The impact of the care system, the acknowledged variability in quality of care across the residential sector and the residential context itself, although at times acknowledged by the social workers, is never seen as anything other than secondary to the agency of the young people.

The social workers expressed frustration with the young people and frequently spoke of them continuing to get into trouble because they had failed to take advantage of assistance or opportunities, which, in their opinions, would be of benefit to them:

> He did have a not very pleasant upbringing, a lot of domestic violence with mum and dad... He has night terrors, or used to do.

Bad nightmares. But again, he's never worked with anybody, so he can work through these things. And he doesn't want to. He doesn't want anger management; he doesn't want to ... discuss any of the things he went through. And as you get older, the chances are less and less. It needs to be done early. And yet, when you speak to him, he's a right nice lad. It's a shame that he is where he is. But how you turn that around, I don't know. Only Tom will be able to do that. (Social Worker)

McLeod (2007, p.278) argues that, 'true listening to disaffected young people ... demands an acceptance that the adult agenda may be flawed and a willingness to consider alternative possibilities'. Nonetheless, expectations that the young person should work to sort out their own 'problems', coupled with incomprehension at their failure to engage with the people who were trying to 'help' them, were prevalent. Such expectations on the part of social workers often seemed to go hand in hand with the absence of any real, productive relationship with the young people, inherent in both the case-management approach to intervention where key tasks are undertaken by numerous junior colleagues/partner agencies/residential unit staff, and a system where social workers seemed to change on a fairly regular basis:

I think I've had about four or five different social workers. That's a bit of a joke, really. Cos you get comfortable with one and they swap. You've got to build a relationship with the other one, then they swap again, and it's awkward. (Robbie, 17)

In addition, for many individuals in residential children's homes, the 'distance' inherent in such relationships is also geographical, as they all too frequently live at a distance from their responsible local authority. It is perfectly understandable that young people might fail to appreciate the relevance of and resist an agenda set by a professional with whom he or she may have had little or no meaningful contact. Indeed, McLeod (2007) argues that:

Reaching an understanding of the viewpoint of a marginalized young person is a time consuming business requiring the sustained relationship central to the traditional notion of case work ... Using relationships positively may be beyond the reach of the office-based 'care manager', focused on paperwork and performance indicators, who has no time for direct involvement with the young people on their caseload. (McLeod, 2007, p.285)

Certainly, such provision hardly seems to be conducive to the establishment of an understanding, trusting and productive relationship between social workers and young people, a state of affairs which has the potential to be further compounded by the numerous professionals with whom they come into contact from the care and youth justice systems:

> The problem for our young people is that there's so many people involved in their lives, and they get a lot of mixed messages ... everybody uses different tactics. (Residential Care Worker)

Nevertheless, the social workers placed responsibility for continued in-care offending firmly at the young people's doorstep and as a consequence of this, it was felt that involvement with the youth justice system could serve as a 'wake-up call' to the 'realities' of life, and possibly deter future misbehaviour. That such perceptions were not borne out by subsequent recidivism rates does not seem to have diminished their potency and undoubtedly influenced their responses to the young people:

> I'm going to be old-fashioned here and just say that to my mind, they're very lenient. And really, sometimes, that short, sharp, shock, they need on occasions. They have to have that, because otherwise everybody would just do as they want to do ... I think even before they get to the courts ... there is a lot of work being done with the young person to try and ... encourage them along the right path ... With the freedom we all of us have, we have to have responsibilities. (Social Worker)

Such perceptions are clearly reflective of the authoritarian agenda, with its theme of children taking responsibility for their own actions, which has come to dominate UK policy and practice. In this way, it has been argued that, 'social phenomena are ... reduced to individual acts and orientations ... rather than as outcomes of complex relationships, structures and influences' (Such and Walker, 2005, p.44). It is little wonder, in light of such discourse, that the social workers should hold these perceptions and that the young people often blame themselves for their situations. Of course, it is not the intention of this book to suggest that young people lack agency and should therefore be allowed to offend and misbehave with impunity. However, simply focusing upon the behaviour and actions of the young people and their families enables other contributory factors relating to policy, procedure and professional practice to be unhelpfully obscured and side-lined.

Indeed, soon after moving from a placement where she felt settled and happy, to a new children's home, Emma was prosecuted for assaulting another resident. When writing her Pre-Sentence Report (PSR), the author (a Youth Offending Team probation officer) assessed that a large part of the reason for both her current and previous offending, was a response to the changes and uncertainty caused by an unwanted move to a new placement:

> Emma has tended to offend when she has been struggling to cope with change and uncertainty in her life, over which she has little personal control and in a specific context. This pattern has emerged again in the recent offences. (PSR: 14.5.08: Offence Analysis)

However, the solution put forward to the youth court is as follows:

> Emma is now able to accept that she does have a problem with anger management and has taken the step of asking her social worker for help with this issue. If she is able to progress with this aspect of her behaviour, then the risk of offending should be much reduced. (PSR: 14.5.08: Conclusion)

It is noticeable that rather than considering how systemic contributions to offending behaviour can be also tackled, the solution put forward by the PSR author reflects the dominant discourse of individual responsibility. This is not a criticism of the author, who was simply doing her job as required under the auspices of current policy and practice, and indeed, when discussing perceptions of young people who offend, Smith argues that simplistic and one-sided conceptualisations of childhood lie at the heart of many recent policy initiatives:

> Offending is seen only as an 'individualised' activity, for which the young people concerned must accept exclusive responsi- bility... Thus policy change is driven by a stereotypical image of the 'dangerous, wilful and agentive' child (Such and Walker, 2005, p.44), whose behaviour need not be understood, but must simply be controlled. (2009b, p.252)

Although the systemic deficiencies, which undoubtedly contributed to Emma's feelings of anger and subsequent behaviour, are acknowl- edged, the ultimate responsibility for sorting out any 'problem' is placed firmly at the door of the fifteen- year-old girl. Certainly, such a perspective offers the professionals and their agencies, a degree of self-preservation: after all, a focus upon the individual responsibility of young people means that the system into which they become enmeshed, and by implication the professionals and their agencies, cannot be so readily blamed for poor outcomes in a society where the media are only too willing to proffer further simplistic explanations in their often reactionary and unhelpful vilification of workers when things go wrong.

A further reason for the willingness of the social workers to embrace the individualisation of troublesome behaviour could lie in frustration stemming both from their inability to effect behav- ioural change in the context of the case-management approach, and budgetary constraints which might mean that they are unable to act in what they perceive to be the child's best interests. Layder (2004, p.96) argues that pride and self esteem are invested in being in control and dealing with things effectively and consequently, a failure to do this might result in the young people being blamed partly as a 'self-defence' mechanism at both a personal and profes- sional level.

Nevertheless, reasons behind individualisation appear to run much deeper than simple frustration, and the perception of the young people being 'dangerous, wilful and agentive' (Such and Walker, 2005, p.44) is also reflected in the incomprehension exhibited by some of the professionals when they described their behaviour. For example, James' social worker frequently expressed frustration and a degree of bafflement at his actions, which, to her, did not make sense:

> I don't know…It's hard to understand him…What he was thinking, I don't know. (Social Worker)

While at one level, this indicates the absence of a positive and productive relationship between social worker and young person, perhaps again relating to the case-management approach to intervention, the perception that the young people are somehow 'different' was expressed on a number of occasions:

> They don't go to school, but you could say, 'What's Susan's car number?' And he'd tell you…But ask him what four plus four is, and he hasn't got a clue! They're just different people, some of these. (Leaving Care Worker)

This perception is undoubtedly, in part, due to the variations between the social backgrounds and experiences of the professionals and the young people and the fact that the young people had developed identities and outlooks which did not accord with the professional's views of 'normal' childhood behaviour. Certainly, as illustrated below, the young people were at times considered too 'knowing':

> They can't teach them anything because they're all street wise. (Leaving Care Worker)

The fact that the children and young people had knowledge which, from the dominant western bourgeois discourse of childhood, was considered to be outside what would normally be associated with this age group, was a clear cause for concern for many. When discussing the concept of the 'underclass', Muncie (2000, p.21) highlights how those on the left have pointed out that a succession of such labels has been consistently attached to the poorest members of society in order to mark them out as either politically dangerous or as marginal outsiders, including, as discussed previously, the 'dangerous classes' and 'social outcasts' of the nineteenth century. Hendrick (2006, pp.8–9) argues that delinquents are 'a convenient 'Other', who are presented to us as a constant reminder of how precarious and fragile our apparently civilised values are and, therefore, of the need for constant surveillance, discipline and punishment'. Certainly, many of the workers I interviewed seemed to feel that greater control, surveillance and punishment was required in order keep the young people under control and to eventually make them into 'conforming adult citizens' (Smith, 2009b, p.252).

Such attitudes have direct, negative implications for how young people in children's homes are responded to by those charged with their care when they get into trouble, with a punitive and retributive outlook predominating when other actions directed towards encouraging the individual young person to change appear to have failed. This will be explored further in Chapter 7 when the issue of how challenging behaviour in the residential context is responded to is discussed in greater detail.

Conclusion

Overall, it is clear that for the young people interviewed, pre-care factors were significant in explaining their in-care involvement in the youth justice system. There is little doubt that experiences of abuse and/or neglect, family examples of criminality, compounded by socio-economic disadvantage, meant that they developed certain outlooks and coping strategies which laid the foundations for challenging and offending behaviour whilst in residential care. The desire for social recognition amongst their peers was particularly important as a means of overcoming other sources of disempowerment and, as will be explored in the following chapter, peer relationships continued to be extremely influential when the young people later entered residential care. Nevertheless, as touched upon in Emma's case, the young people also frequently alluded to experiences directly related to the care system and the residential context, which provided additional explanations for 'offending' behaviour. While acknowledged by the professionals, these factors were not prioritised in their responses. The following chapters will therefore go on to explore and analyse the contribution of the young people's in-care experiences to youth justice contact.

5
Solidarity, Conflict and the Residential Regime

Introduction

Research has revealed that there is a predominance of crisis admission into care for adolescents, often following a breakdown in family relationships (ADCS, 2013) and this was certainly the case for the majority of young people who participated in this study. Indeed, as a result of experiences within their families of origin, and the often subsequent breakdown of placements with other family members and/or foster carers, the young people were eventually placed in residential care. The following chapter will explore how they perceived their challenging and offending behaviour to have been influenced by factors within the residential context. Continuing a theme explored in the previous chapter, the impact of peer relations in residential care will be seen to be of particular importance, with the desire for social recognition an ever present factor. Nevertheless, as concluded by previous research (Sinclair and Gibbs, 1998), the young people's behaviour was also very much a product of their immediate environment, including the culture of individual children's homes and associated interactions between staff and residents. These themes will be explored with particular reference to the importance of power dynamics in residential care.

The perceptions of professionals from the care and youth justice systems will also be included at certain points with a view to offering further insights, particularly regarding how their attitudes and consequent actions might impact either positively or negatively upon the behaviour of the young people.

Reactions to entering residential care

Goffman (1961, pp.61–63) found that inmates of institutions employ various tactics in order to cope with or adapt to the situation in which they find themselves. First, there is the tack of 'situational withdrawal', where the inmate withdraws apparent attention from everything except events immediately around his body and sees these in a perspective not employed by others present. Secondly, there is the 'intransigent line' where the inmate intentionally challenges the institution by flagrantly refusing to cooperate with staff. These are examples of resistance to the power of the system (Foucault, 1978). Other tactics include 'conversion' and 'colonization', where the individual makes the best of what the institution has to offer or goes a step further, embracing the values of the institution. When asked to describe their feelings about being taken into care, the responses of the young people varied. Some described being unhappy at first, but then came to accept their situation after a period of adjustment:

> Didn't have any say in the decision. Weren't happy. Police put me there, I couldn't go home... Didn't know where I was, who I was with, what I was supposed to do. They just chuck you in with a load of people you don't know... I was scared at first, but then I weren't bothered. (Mark, 20)

> It were ok. I were worried at first, but then I got used to it. (Lucy, 17)

> I didn't like it when I first went in... because they're not your parents. They couldn't tell me what to do. But after a couple of months, I got on with them. (Peter, 20)

Here, Mark, Lucy and Peter appear to have utilised the tactics of conversion and colonisation to varying degrees. However, a young woman spoke of feeling overwhelmed when she was first taken into care and placed in a large residential unit with approximately 11 other young people:

> I didn't like it... I don't like it when it's busy anyway... You don't get a choice though: they put you anywhere. (Sarah, 18)

As a consequence of this, Sarah misbehaved to such an extent that she was quickly moved on to another placement. This is clearly an example of the intransigent line being utilised to achieve a desired effect. Robbie did not agree with the decision to place him in care, and consequently refused to engage in the life of the numerous homes in which he became resident:

> I never used to follow the rules ... They had certain rules, but I was never there, so I wasn't bothered. If I did end up staying there for whatever reason, if I couldn't get back to (my home town), or whatever, I'd just do my own thing, just sit in my room and watch TV or something, or go out. (Robbie, 17)

Here, Robbie employs the strategy of situational withdrawal, albeit to a much lesser degree than that described by Goffman (1961). Undoubtedly, for many of the young people, this appears to have been a time in their lives when they felt out of control and out of their depth and reacted accordingly. However, some young people described advantages of being taken into care:

> I liked it better. Because I got on with me mam better. (Jack, 22)

> I think that it were better ... I knew all people that were in there. (Daniel, 18)

Nevertheless, it was the case that the young people's feelings about being taken into care, did not necessarily seem to have an impact upon whether they got into trouble while in care. As previously described, Robbie disagreed with the decision to place him in care, and continued to offend throughout his many placements. However, while other young people described positive feelings about being taken into care, or adjusting to their situation and coming to appreciate the positive aspects, as will be discussed in the next section, this did not necessarily result in a cessation of offending/troublesome behaviour.

Deterioration of behaviour

Although most of the young people had experienced some degree of involvement with the youth justice system prior to entering residential care, a number described how their behaviour deteriorated further when they began living in a children's home:

> It just got worse from there, when I first went into care ... Offending got worse. I'd been to prison once before I got put in care, then I got out of prison and I was doing alright for a little bit, and then I

started offending again and I got put in care and got another three prison sentences. (John, 18)

Started getting worse when I went into care ... We used to go into the back garden and stuff and get pissed, and to this lass's house, and one night we had a couple of drinks and that, and went into the kitchen and got done on a burglary charge. (David, 18)

Indeed, in Jack's case, although he had previously been engaged in 'risky' behaviour and 'soft' drug use, he did not have any official involvement with the youth justice system until after entering residential care:

It was while I was living at (the children's home) that I got sent down for the first time. (Jack, 22)

The young people's explanations pointed to a number of possible reasons for this which included being placed with other, often older, young people who were involved in criminal activities:

I was mixing with worse people ... The sort of people that had been in prison themselves. They put me in a care home at 12, with guys that were 16 and 17 ... There was this guy there on Class A drugs and that ... I was just with gangs, smoking weed, graffiti, on the streets and that. (John, 18)

These findings are in accordance with previous research (Darker, Ward and Caulfield, 2008; Stewart et al., 1994) and indeed, a constant theme reported by Taylor (2006) in the context of her study, was the pre-existence of a delinquent subculture in residential care: 'in other words, there is always a crowd to follow' (ibid., p.88). Although the peer group in residential care has been found to be a valuable source of support in certain contexts (Emond, 2003), Polsky's (1962) classic study graphically illustrates the power of an unchecked delinquent sub-culture to impact negatively upon certain residents. This might well have been a reason why for some, offending behaviour often continued or even increased, despite being removed to different settings. As discussed earlier, the desire to fit in with peers and the acquisition of social recognition through offending can be a powerful factor, especially in situations where the young people might otherwise feel out of control; certainly, Emond (2003, p.324) argues that 'for young people in children's homes the significance of their relationships with their fellow residents should not be underestimated'.

John also described getting into trouble after being introduced to 'criminally involved' young people from the local communities in which the care homes were situated, by fellow residents:

> It's kids from inside the care homes that know people from outside the care home ... When I moved to Coalton, I didn't know anyone from around there. And then, I started hanging around with all their mates, and there was a gang of them, like 20-people ... But they only used to do bad things, though. They just used to introduce you to bad people really. (John, 18)

Of course, as delinquency had characterised many of the young people's lives prior to them entering the homes, it could consequently be argued that their behaviour was simply a continuation of existing patterns. Indeed, in the context of their research, Sinclair and Gibbs (1998) commented that criticism, if it were merited, was that the homes had not protected the residents against the local delinquent culture, not that they had increased its temptations. Indeed current education secretary Michael Gove recently expressed his concern about the number of children's homes which are located in high crime areas (Topping, 2013). This is something to which careful thought should be given when placing potentially vulnerable young people. It is also the case that growing older is in itself significant in terms of the onset of offending, with a peak age for both sexes having been found to be at 14 or 15 (Farrington, 1995; Rutter,, Giller and Hagell, 1998). Therefore, as the majority of young people who enter contemporary children's homes fall into this age group, it could arguably be that their age is as much a contributory factor as location and placement. Nevertheless, it certainly appears to be the case that in some instances, the young people's behaviour worsened and for others, residence in a children's home precipitated contact with the youth justice system where there had been none before.

Another reason given for the worsening or continuation of offending or troublesome behaviour was a perceived lack of control by residential staff over the whereabouts and behaviour of residents:

> I got worse, actually. Because there were nobody telling me what to do... In a kid's home, if one of carers said no to you, they can't tell you no, they can't tell you not to do stuff. They can't slap your wrist or slap your arse and send you to bed, or nowt. They can't tell you what to do. It's different. They can tell me to not go out and give me advice, but they can't say, 'You're not allowed to do this; you're not allowed to do that.' You can just tell em to fuck off; they can't do nowt really to you. (Lucy, 17)

> You're allowed to do whatever you want. Well, not allowed to, but they can't ground you and stuff like that... They daren't ground me anyway, because I'd just go. (Tom, 15)

These comments accord with the findings of earlier research, such as that undertaken by Taylor (2006) in which there was general consensus amongst the young people that there was very little staff could do to control residents, who were usually well aware of that fact. These concerns are reflected in the comments made by many of the professionals, a number of whom felt that the inability of staff and homes to control their residents was a major precipitating factor in offending, and that the young people now had too much power in those circumstances. This theme will be returned to in Chapter 7.

Solidarity with other residents

The allure of peer relationships and maintaining a valued reputation was again illustrated by participants who described initially doing well in a particular residential placement, only for their behaviour to deteriorate with the arrival of other young people. For example, David describes his residential care placement in very positive terms, especially with regard to relationships he developed with staff and the developmental opportunities provided. However, when another young person came to live in the home, he could not resist getting into trouble with him. The relationship and need to fit in with his peer/s was more important than the need to please staff and to conform to what was considered to be acceptable behaviour:

> When 'Terry Jones' came, I started smoking blow and stuff. Then the burglary happened … I went along with it. (David, 18)

John described similar experiences:

> But then … cos all the other kids are like that as well, cheeky with the staff, I just wanted to go along with it. (John, 18)

Sinclair and Gibbs (1998) found that residents were not happier if they said they got on well with staff or if they reported that they had had a lot of help from the home. Rather, it was the resident group and how they got on with them that seemed to make the difference. In many ways, this is to be expected given the fact that staff come and go on a shift basis, whereas the resident group are a more constant presence. It undoubtedly also relates to previous experiences where, for the reasons described, the peer group came to replace immediate family, and adult influence, in terms of providing emotional support and a sense of self worth and status.

The need to display solidarity with another resident was cited by James as a reason for getting into trouble. James described how he received his first prison sentence at the age of fourteen for assaulting a member of staff in a residential placement, who he felt was unfairly restraining another resident:

> He were restraining this lad on the floor, and this lad said, 'Get off me', and he wouldn't get off him, so I ran up to him, I pushed him off and my knee hit him in the nose and I broke his nose. And I got done for that. I got six months for that. (James, 16)

Similarly, Robbie was also prosecuted after involving himself in an incident with another resident who was in an altercation with members of staff:

> Something happened in the care home involving one of the other lads that were there. Like, the staff, I'd say, assaulted him, know what I mean? Obviously like, he was my mate, so I got involved in that. (Robbie, 17)

When seeking to explain such solidarity, Goffman (1961) states that:

> More important as a reorganizing influence is the fraternalization process, through which socially distant persons find themselves developing mutual support and common counter-mores in opposition to a system that has forced them into intimacy and into a single, equalitarian community of fate. (Goffman, 1961, p.57)

It seems inevitable that young people who have been removed from their families and existing support networks to placements which are unfamiliar and undoubtedly daunting might seek to form alliances with other residents. It is entirely possible that they might develop loyalties to the resident group, in opposition to staff, who could be viewed as part of the 'establishment' and enforcers of the system. This is in line with Foucault's assertion that where there is power, there is also resistance and indeed other forms of resistance have been documented in residential contexts. For example, Frost, Mills and Stein (1999) report that one of the authors had witnessed a unit where the young people developed an entire secret language which had the effect of excluding staff from their interactions.

Solidarity between residents also extended to the arrival of newcomers to the unit, as evidenced by Lucy, who described being prosecuted for the first time, after becoming involved in an incident between her friend and a new girl:

> That new girl hit one of my mates who were in kids home ... so my reaction ... is to jump in and stop it. But I think I got that mad because of what she'd done, I like, took it to another proportion. (Lucy, 17)

This account accords with earlier research conducted by Kilpatrick et al. (2008), which found that the potential for peer conflict was further exacerbated when a newcomer was introduced to the group. It also chimes with research undertaken by Barter et al. (2004), who found that with regard to peer violence in the residential context, girls often reported isolated and sporadic attacks in response to a specific trigger.

Nevertheless, there also appeared to be a degree of self-preservation in their actions, with young people not wanting to suffer the consequences of being seen to be complicit with the system against fellow residents. Indeed, in his study of residential treatment for 'delinquent adolescents', Polsky (1962) found that a delinquent subculture flourished which stressed intimidation through physical coercion, toughness and a code of silence and endured even though the central actors changed periodically. Certainly, in the context of the current research, some felt that they had little choice other than to display solidarity:

> I could have grassed them up, but that would just have got me in trouble, because if they didn't get sent down for it, then I've still got to live with them. So you can't do things like that when you're a kid, because you get beat up for it. (John, 18)

Here, John clearly and consciously acted in his own self interest rather than from an innate sense of loyalty to his fellow residents and in fact Goffman (1961, p.60) argues that although there are solidarising tendencies such as fraternalisation and clique formation, they are limited, and that constraints which place inmates/residents in a position to sympathise and communicate with each other do not necessarily lead to high group morale and solidarity. Certainly, although solidarity might have been displayed against staff or newcomers, relationships between fellow residents were at times precarious.

Conflict with other residents

Barter (2008) reports that peer violence has been consistently highlighted by young people in residential care as one of their overriding concerns, and provides a useful summary of relevant research: Morris and Wheatley (1994) found behaviour ranging from teasing or being picked on, to physical attacks, and Utting (1997) reports that, 'possibly half the total of abuse reported in institutions is peer abuse'. Research conducted by Wade et al. (1998) indicates the extent to which running away is related to unhappiness with peers, while Sinclair and Gibbs (1998) report that nearly half (44 per cent) of the 223 young people interviewed in their research stated that they had been bullied during their stay at the homes. In the context of her own research (Barter et al. 2004), Barter (2008) reports that four different forms of peer violence were derived from the young people's accounts, including direct physical assault, physical 'non-contact' attacks, verbal abuse and unwelcome sexual behaviours. Similarly, in this research, young people described how the police become involved as the result of physical conflicts with fellow residents in the homes:

> I had this CD and he thought it were his, thought he could try and start. He offered me out, so I stood up and put the blade to his throat. (Tom, 15)

> There was one lad who got on my nerves. He was a wind up merchant. I smacked him about three times, and every time they called the police. (Mark, 20)

> Got into argument over a Play-Station; assaulted other lad. They called police. (Peter, 20)

As illustrated by these accounts, an impression was sometimes conveyed by the young people of having to project an image which indicated that they were capable of standing up for themselves, and, at times, prove this by physical action. A failure to do this could result in bullying. Only one young person, Sarah, an eighteen-year-old woman with learning difficulties, specifically described being the victim of bullying, while the other young people seemed keen to stress that they had been able to stand up for themselves:

> I'm quite a confident person, and I think I stood up for myself when I went in. (Lucy, 17)

The need to project a 'tough' image could in part be an extension of the 'working class' cultural backgrounds of the young people, in which a certain degree of machismo is seen as desirable. Certainly, with regard to incidents of low-level physical violence reported in their research, Barter et al. (2004) found that boys used this form of violence to publicly present a particular kind of 'macho' or 'hard' masculinity to their male peers. Therefore, the young people's behaviour in the homes could simply be an extension of previous behaviour in their 'home world' peer groups, perhaps amplified by the exigencies of the residential environment. Similarly, those who were previously vulnerable to bullying, such as Sarah, continued to be so after their entry to residential care. Indeed, Sinclair and Gibbs (1998) found that for many, experiences of being bullied were a continuation of experiences prior to entry to residential care.

Residential hierarchies: the 'pecking order'

Nevertheless, there is little doubt that the young people also responded specifically to the residential environment. Kilpatrick et al. (2008) found that the hierarchies of peer groups and the negotiating of position within the group were ever-present sources of disruptive behaviour or peer violence in the residential context and similarly, the notion of the 'pecking order' was something which was commented upon by a number of professionals in this study:

> You always seem to get a pecking order established in residential homes ... Youngster's kind of wanting to view themselves as being the most tough, if you like. (Children's Home Manager)

> We've had one young person, who, as soon as he came in, said, 'Right, I'm going to be top dog in here!' He got involved in a bit of crime ... but for him, it was something quite good, because he was seen as top dog. (Residential Worker)

> They either fit in, or they don't stay there long. They usually move on ... It is a kind of bullying, but not bullying as such. They're sort of put in their place, know what I mean? I have first choice and then you can come. (Leaving Care Worker)

While research has found that support and help from other young people, getting to know young people from different backgrounds and having young people to share interests and activities with were important to many and considered to be some of the best things about living in a children's home (Morgan, 2009; Emond, 2003). Morgan (2009) also found that many of the young people described having to live with people they did not get on with as one of the worst things about living in a children's home. This could well result in a greater potential for friction between the young people and consequent police involvement. Some of the professionals interviewed felt that the emergence of smaller homes had resulted in a reduction of such problems. Nevertheless, as will be explored in the following chapter, it became apparent that residence in smaller establishments is not without its difficulties.

Culture and characteristics of children's homes

As with previous research (Whitaker et al., 1998; Sinclair and Gibbs, 1998; Berridge and Brodie, 1998; Brown et al., 1998; Hicks et al., 2007; Anglin, 2002) the potential for the culture and characteristics of individual homes to impact upon outcomes was clearly illustrated by the study. Most of the young people reported a range of positive and negative experiences across different placements in both the local authority and private sectors (see also Berridge and Brodie, 1998) and it was apparent that the exercise of power within homes can be an important contributory factor to the precipitation or otherwise of challenging and disruptive behaviour.

The disempowering effects of institution-oriented practices were commented upon by a number of the young people: John described how his girlfriend had been arrested after becoming frustrated when refused a drink of water by staff after a certain time of night:

> She's still asking for a drink, saying, 'Listen, I've got a dry mouth, I've got no spit, you can't refuse me a drink of water', and all the time, they were being that funny, they said, 'No', so she threw cup down the stairs and she got arrested for it! (John, 18)

Goffman (1961, p.45) argues that one of the most telling ways in which an individual's 'economy of action' can be disrupted is the obligation to request permission for supplies for minor activities that she or he can execute on her or his own on the outside – this puts the individual in a submissive or suppliant role. It is little wonder that under such circumstances, the young people might become frustrated and rebel against what could be viewed as unfair curtailments to their freedom. Robbie, who reported having experienced a great of personal freedom whilst with his family, expressed particular dissatisfaction with residential life:

> Like, you can't eat after 10 o'clock. You've got to get out of the lounge at 10 o'clock, no TVs on. You couldn't have music on after

10 o'clock in your room. Just stupid rules, really. You couldn't go in other people's rooms and chill. Just daft rules. If I invite someone into my room and something goes missing, it's my responsibility…I said that to (the manager), and he said, 'That's not the reason.' I said, 'What is the reason, then?' and he never explained it, so I just couldn't be bothered with it…In Coalton, it was set (meal) times, and that…So, if you didn't get in for the time, they'd try saying, 'You're not having any tea.' I'd be kicking off about that. (Robbie, 17)

Robbie clearly felt that his views were not being respected and that those in charge would not engage with him in terms of explaining the rules of the home and the justifications for them being in place. As previously discussed, many of the young people appear, in their pre-care family circumstances, to have experienced a degree of freedom and autonomy, not traditionally associated with conventional notions of childhood. Having formed an identity and participated in a certain lifestyle prior to entering a children's home, some then experienced great difficulty in adjusting to the more conventional requirements of certain residential regimes, such as set meal times or an 'age-appropriate' curfew, which could, in turn, be a potential source of conflict. Indeed, such difficulties were alluded to by some of the professionals:

They come into our care, and obviously, they've got behavioural problems. It could be lack of boundaries, house rules. So when they do come into our care, we make sure that we put house rules in place…We explain the children's guide to them, and they have to follow house rules…Sometimes, it takes a few weeks for them to get used to the house rules and boundaries…It's a struggle, but we know that in a few weeks that will be over-turned, and that cycle will be broken, because at the end of the day, no matter what age they are…they still need boundaries. (Children's Home Manager)

In certain respects it is understandable and proper that young people living in a residential context (as in a 'conventional' home) should have to abide by certain expectations in terms of conduct and behaviour. Indeed those charged with running such establishments are often required to consider the welfare of a number of young people, perhaps of varying ages, all of whom might have differing needs. For example, a requirement that music is not played after 10 p.m. by the older young people in order that the younger residents or those with early morning school commitments can sleep does not, from an objective standpoint, seem unreasonable. However, the impression was sometimes conveyed by the young people that certain rules were imposed without explanation or applied in a rigid fashion which did not take individual needs and perspectives into account. Indeed, the Residential Unit Manager quoted previously (and below) speaks of the imposition of 'house rules', rather than how life within the residential context might be negotiated between residents and staff and reveals a potentially unhelpful negative 'them and us' perception of the young people:

> If you let them walk all over you, they will. (Children's Home Manager)

The requirement of set mealtimes in certain homes, while undoubtedly well intentioned (see McIntosh et al., 2011), was a particular bone of contention for some and seems to be an example of something which could be negotiated between staff and individual residents in a way which takes into account their previous experiences, feelings and current needs. Indeed, recommendations produced by previous research (King, Raynes and Tizard, 1973; Whitaker, Archer and Hicks, 1998; Clough, 2000; Berridge, 2002) emphasise that results in children's homes are best where young people are accorded respect as individuals and effective relationships are built between staff and young people which take into account the children's perspective. Clough (2000, pp.88–90) in particular argues that in effect, the experience of the resident should be at the heart of practice. The factors that he contends are intrinsic to resident-centred practice include: an attempt to understand the resident, daily life within the home being built from an attempt to produce systems that best match residents' wants and needs, time being made within the daily routine to listen to individual residents and residents being involved in negotiations about life in the establishment. Indeed, O'Sullivan (2011, p.44) argues that:

> If people feel that workers have not consulted them or given them an opportunity to influence decisions or imposed a decision on them or not fully explained one to them, they are less likely to

become positively involved in its implementation. It is understandable that in such situations service users may become uncooperative or actively sabotage plans they have had no part in making.

Certainly, it stands to reason that if children and young people are engaged with in a meaningful way which accords with their individual levels of maturity and comprehension they will be more likely to understand, cooperate and be happy with residential life. Nevertheless, many of the young people did not feel that they were engaged with in certain placements, which as Robbie described, created frustration and resentment. It was also highlighted how residence in different institutions can perpetuate difficulties:

> A lot of them might have been in care for a long time. And obviously, different homes have different house rules. They might have been able to get away with it at the other place, but they can't get away with it here. So it does take a while for them to get used to the house rules. (Children's Home Manager)

This was something of particular relevance to many of the participants in this study who were at times moved on either for financial reasons or because they got into trouble. As will be explored further in the following chapter, such movement has the potential to be extremely damaging and precipitate further challenging behaviour.

Staff-resident relationships

Inextricably linked to the culture and characteristics of individual homes is the way in which staff interact with the young people. These relationships can provide the most positive experiences of care, but also have the potential to be both damaging and destructive (Kendrick, 2012). When asked about their relationships with and perceptions of staff, most of the young people reported a range of both positive and negative experiences. Some felt that staff were well-meaning and tried their best, but that at the time, it did not make any difference to how they behaved:

> All the workers I had tried their best, but it was just me that was out of control. There was nothing else they could do. They couldn't

tie me up or do anything, but they always encouraged me to do the right thing, and I just never listened. (John, 18)

Staff were decent people, but got treated like shit, sometimes by me, sometimes by other residents. They tried to help us as much as they could. I think I was a pain in the arse anyway...I didn't care about anyone else, except myself. I was a little shit. (Mark, 20)

To a certain extent, these accounts tie in with the negative self image presented by many of the young people, in which self-blame was prevalent. Rather like their accounts of why they were taken into care, the young people seem to have imbibed the negative comments made about them, forming the belief that they were the ones who failed to do the right thing and be appropriately grateful for the help that was provided. Nevertheless, their accounts do provide an insight into the challenges faced by staff, many of whom, according to the young people, endeavoured to be a positive influence:

I bonded quite close with quite a few of the staff. They're like me mum and dad to me, not like carers, if you know what I mean...They do help a lot, staff. (Lucy, 17)

The staff and that were alright, good laugh and that...It were good. (David, 18)

Certainly, in their research, Sinclair and Gibbs (1998) noted that, as by most measures, staff were considered good or caring; there was little to separate homes in this respect. However, Sarah described feeling frustrated and sometimes lashing out because she felt that she was getting mixed messages from the staff group:

The staff were dickheads...They did my head in. One used to say one thing, another summat else...One took pocket money off me, another didn't. (Sarah, 18)

This could relate to an absence of the type of strong, purposeful leadership which has been found to engender positive outcomes (Whitaker Archer and Hicks, 1998; Sinclair and Gibbs, 1998; Brown et al., 1998; Anglin, 2002). In addition, the effect of staff movement was touched upon:

There's been a change recently, and he's got a new key worker. And Josh is really, really unsettled by that ... It's had a big effect on him ... He's really pissed off. (Leaving Care Worker)

In Josh's case, his previous Key Worker had not left the unit. However, it had been decided that he should be reallocated to a new staff member, despite the existence of a positive relationship with his current worker. Josh's Leaving Care Worker was not aware of the reason for this. Such seemingly arbitrary changes might engender further feelings of rejection and insecurity amongst the young people, affecting their already low self-esteem; resulting in challenging behaviour. The idea that attachments are important in the prevention of offending was touched upon in Chapter 1 (see also Taylor, 2006) and is clearly resonant in such circumstances.

Other negative experiences were also highlighted, such as when John talked of one particular placement being little more than an exercise in containment:

It weren't nice at all. All the staff there were muppets! There was one guy that I liked ... all the other's, I didn't like them at all. Cos they couldn't be arsed about it. They just used to sit there all day reading their book, while you're sat there, bored, because they weren't talking with you or doing anything with you. You didn't get activities there, or nothing. You just used to be in (the children's home) all day. From there I went to prison. (John, 18)

In her research into offending in residential care Taylor (2006, p.97) highlights how boredom was identified as a cause of 'deviant' behaviour by some and links this to Hirschi's (1969) contention that the more an individual is involved or engrossed in conventional activities, the less time he or she will have to indulge in crime. John's comments also reveal a feeling on his part that some staff did not really care, a perception which was prevalent in Taylor's research and was also expressed by Emma:

They were just there for the money. (Emma, 15)

McNeish, Newman and Roberts (2002, p.276) write of the value of positive and enduring relationships in the residential context, stating that 'an essential ingredient ... was the young person feeling as if the adult genuinely cared – that they were there for them and not just doing their job'. Certainly, the perception that staff do not really care could result in the reinforcement of a negative self image on the part of the young people, while at the same time fostering their previously described reliance upon the peer group for validation and a sense of self-worth. It could also result in them feeling unable to inform staff of bullying or other difficulties. Of course, as discussed earlier, the importance attached to peer group approval by some, might serve to override the value of attachments to staff: nevertheless, as discussed below, staff-resident relationships and interactions *can* be instrumental in the precipitation of both positive and negative outcomes.

Some young people spoke of feeling that staff did not accord them appropriate respect and space or nagged them over trivial things. The impression was conveyed that this sometimes led to unnecessary confrontations and an escalation of incidents which might otherwise have resolved themselves:

> You never get better unless the staff just give you space. Because some care homes are in your face too much, and that's not helping you at all. Not when they're in your face, and they argue back with you. That's just making you more angry. (John, 18)

> Lots of staff deal with it in different ways. When I'm angry, I go upstairs and I lash out in my room. They try talking to me, but I ... just tell them to leave me to it. But, like with other people, when they're arguing, they like, argue back a bit. (Lucy, 17)

Such experiences were also mentioned by some professionals:

> Staff varies. Some of them deal with it in a laid back way, and others react, and there's a situation that then escalates and can lead to an offence. (YOT Worker)

Berridge (2002, p.92) sets out factors that his research suggests characterise good, productive staff-resident relationships. The most effective staff in this respect are informal in approach, easy to talk to, respect young people, listen to what they say, try to understand and not lecture them and are frank and sometimes challenging, rather than 'pushy' and 'nagging'. Kilpatrick et al. also note that the dominant theme running through their study is the fundamental importance of the relationship between the staff and the young people:

> Young people we encountered endorsed the findings from the research review in identifying skilled staff as those who know young people and can therefore anticipate difficult situations, are calm and consistent, can successfully de-escalate situations...listen to young people, take an interest in them...and refrain from playing power games or constantly engaging in verbal battles with them. (2008, p.16)

Indeed, almost identical sentiments were expressed by a professional in the context of the current study:

> The better residential staff...were the ones who could see trouble coming and take diversionary action to stop it. But too often I'm afraid staff get into confrontations that are needless. Nobody's going to win...and it should never get to that...You deal with people in a reasoned way, and you give them due space and respect, and understand where they're coming from. (YOT Worker)

Certainly, in the more positive experiences described in this research, staff appeared to be approachable, and have a willingness to engage with the young people, according them respect as individuals, rather than pursuing an authoritarian line:

> There was one...that was good. The staff in there were more like normal people. They weren't like care workers...The staff in there were just better altogether...They weren't just there to do a job. They acted more...like mates...You could speak to any of them. In the homes, there were certain staff members that you'd get on with better than others...But in there you'd always get on with them all. There was only three of us, but everyone felt the same about the staff. They were alright. (Robbie, 17)

> The best one is Jenny...Because she treats me like a normal person. (Emma, 15)

Carol...understood. She used to treat me like an adult, not like a kid. (Peter, 20)

This suggests that good practice should encourage such aspects of staff-resident interactions and indeed, Stevens and Furnivall (2008, p.200) highlight how discrete therapeutic approaches can reap benefits when working with young people in residential care settings; opportunity-led work (Ward, 2000) or working in the *lifespace* are interventions which have been utilised at various points. Both approaches involve the conscious use of the everyday opportunities that present themselves in residential work, to engage meaningfully with young people about what is happening in their lives. A key aspect of working in the lifespace is the opportunity for the development of close working relationships between young people and staff, with practitioners building up knowledge and understanding of the young people's personal histories in order to make sense of their behaviours in the present (Stevens and Furnivall, 2008). Stevens and Furnivall reveal how the creation of a therapeutic *milieu* by staff is essential in order to implement effective lifespace interventions – this refers to the 'feel' of the unit. As suggested by previous research, a range of factors will impact upon the milieu and might include the physical design, the organisational culture or the composition of resident and staff group (ibid., p.202). Such approaches seem to point to a positive way forward for residential care, a way in which often troubled young people can be worked with in an a way which is both empowering and productive of desirable outcomes.

Conclusion

Overall it is apparent that while peer relations continue to be significant in explaining offending and troublesome behaviour, there is no doubt factors directly related to the residential context also have the capacity to significantly impact upon the propensity of young people to get into trouble. In particular, the differing cultures and characteristics of individual children's homes and associated interactions between staff and residents appear to be capable of producing both positive and negative outcomes; the young people experienced a variation in the quality of provision across both the public and private sector. Good practice requires leadership in developing positive cultures in residential care (Whitaker et al., 1998; Sinclair and Gibbs, 1998; Brown et al., 1998; Anglin, 2002) with 'clarity of roles and congruence in aims and objectives' (Kendrick, 2012, p.296). Rather than pursuing an authoritarian line which can produce resistance (Goffman, 1961; Foucault, 1978, 1977), staff should be approachable and willing to engage with the young people in a way that respects them as individuals, taking into account their personal histories, perspectives and life experiences (Clough, 2000).

6
Instability, Homogeneity and Isolation

Introduction

This chapter will explore and analyse the perceptions of the young people and professionals of how certain aspects of the overall policy framework and practices of the care system relate to and influence offending behaviour. It will begin by exploring the impact of placement movement upon already vulnerable young people and go on to discuss how placement size, homogeneity and location have the potential to engender negative reactions. Certainly, the ideals of corporate parenting seem to be something which the care system all too often fails to uphold with young people often feeling powerless to influence their experiences.

Placement movement: the implications of instability

> I liked it better in Oxley than I do here, because I settled down after everything, and then it were like when I settled down, they just moved me. That's why I can't settle down, because they just keep moving kids because they haven't got enough money. It's all about money... They didn't have the funds to keep me there. (Emma, 15)

The Care Matters agenda (DfES, 2007) identifies stable relationships as one of the key factors in ensuring good outcomes for children in care. Nevertheless, there is still an unacceptable amount of movement for a number of young people, with 11 per cent having had three or more placements in the year ending March 2013 (DfE, 2013c). In the context of this research, young people were sometimes moved on for financial reasons, which had negative consequences in terms of their psychological and emotional well-being and consequent behaviour. Emma (quoted above) had settled into a particular placement, but was then moved because Social Services decided that the placement was no longer suitable for both financial and strategic reasons. Emma proceeded to get into trouble soon after being moved, and her Youth Offending Team case-worker sought to explain why this might have occurred:

> As far as I'm aware, she's never assaulted anybody in the street, or strangers. They've always been part of the structure she's been required to live within, which, for some reason, she's not been able to cope with from time to time…With Emma, most of her offences have happened shortly after she's been moved. So that sort of makes sense to me: a feeling of powerlessness. At the stroke of a pen, somebody can make a decision that completely turns her life inside out. She's got to live somewhere different with a completely different set of people from the previous day, and that must be terribly difficult to cope with. And I think that happened when she was first moved to Bradfield, which is where quite a few of her offences were, and it certainly happened when she came to Coalton. (YOT Worker)

Peter also described offending after being moved away from an 'out of area' placement he liked and back to Coalton, because of financial considerations:

> Because Coalton was too tight to sort the money out…I didn't take no drugs there. It was good. But Social Services thought I'd be better off in Coalton…My opinion wasn't taken into consideration. (Peter, 20)

Similarly, a solicitor spoke of his experience with a young person who re-offended after being returned to a residential children's home in the Coalton area from a placement in which he had blossomed:

> He was a nightmare and a PYO (persistent young offender), and he got placed …in Bradfield, and they basically said, 'He's fantastic'.

> He went from non-attendance at school, to attending 100 per cent. He was being polite, he didn't get into trouble, he did everything, and Coalton just said, 'Sorry, we can't afford to pay for this. We're not paying for anybody living in Bradfield.' They withdrew the funding. (Solicitor)

Such findings are consistent with those highlighted in the National Care Association report, *Every Budget Matters* (2009), which surveyed staff at 100 care homes and residential care providers and found that almost half of the sample said that they did not trust current commissioning structures to be making decisions that were in the best interests of the child. Many gave examples of where children and young people, outside of the remit of their care plan, had been moved out of stable placements where they were happy and doing well. It was stated that, 'such moves were blatantly financially led, or in response to local changes in placement strategy or services' (ibid., p.7).

In this way young people experience an often damaging lack of stability and under such circumstances, it is little wonder that they might exhibit challenging behaviour and struggle to trust the adults who are charged with their care. These experiences seem to have conveyed the message to some of the young people that their feelings and welfare were of less importance than financial considerations, which could potentially result in a further diminution of their often already low self-esteem and manifest in their responses.

Placement movement also occurred when a young person presented persistently challenging behaviour:

> The manager don't want me there no more, cos I cause trouble. Loads of stuff, cops always coming; costing them loads of money, and stuff like that... The thing is, they got me settled in and then moved me. I kind of got used to it. I weren't bothered. Made friends, and they moved me. (Tom, 15)

> I just used to get arrested and then, when I was in the police station, find out that I was moving somewhere else. I don't know if they had a meeting about it. Went to the police station and said, 'Where am I moving to again?' It was a regular thing. Get arrested and move somewhere else. (Robbie, 17)

Usually, unless they presented particular risks to themselves or others, the young people were initially accommodated in foster care or (much less frequently) a local authority residential placement, depending upon perceived needs and/or risks. However, if their behaviour continued to be considered challenging and/or 'risky', they were then moved on to a succession of usually private placements in various parts of the country. John goes on to describe how such movement had impacted upon him:

> You could never get settled; you've not got a straight head ever, because you're being moved everywhere, meeting new people. They need to put you somewhere where you're going to settle and try and get out of trouble, and try and get help constantly, instead of just moving me around constantly...Maybe if they didn't move me around everywhere, I wouldn't have ended up as bad as I did. (John, 18)

John's comments echo the point made by Clough, Bullock and Ward who argue that:

> A child doing badly in residential care needs a good-quality intervention, not transfer to another...home. System neglect, whereby the needs of children remain unmet, is less obvious than physical or sexual abuse but is no less dangerous. (2006, p.44)

Indeed, Munro and Hardy (2007) highlight how in response to abusive and neglectful parenting or multiple care givers, children may develop psychological defences to cope with anxiety and distress which in turn can cause the development of internal working models that impair their ability to relate to others in the future (Howe, 2005). Given the experiences of abuse and/or neglect endured by many of the young people in this research in their families of origin, it is hardly surprising that they might go on to experience difficulties in forming bonds with subsequent care-givers and settling into residential life. That the response of the care system to challenging behaviour or financial deficits is more often than not to move them on to another placement is short-sighted in the extreme. Certainly, Munro and Hardy conclude that:

> Placement instability further reduces the opportunity for children to develop permanent, secure attachments (Leathers, 2002) and may compound existing difficulties and further reinforcement of

insecure patterns of attachment. Children are less likely to attempt to establish intimate relationships with future carers and more likely to display behaviour that keeps carers emotionally distant. Such maladaptive coping techniques and apparently challenging behaviour may lead to placement breakdowns and further rejection. (2007, pp.2–3)

The accounts of the professionals in this study unfortunately confirmed that such negative consequences occurred all too frequently amongst the young people in their care:

> We're getting youngsters at the age of 13, 14, who I've known have had up to 39 placements, prior to coming here. So you're looking at attachment issues; massive distrust of adults has already set in, no stability whatsoever. (Children's Home Manager)

The notion of young people sabotaging placements through fear of forming attachments and then being rejected again after so many moves was also mentioned by some of the professionals, and has disturbing implications for their future emotional and social health and well-being; indeed, Tom seems to be an example of this:

> Everywhere it's happened, everywhere, even in here (in a Young Offender's Institution). A month I'm good for when I first come in, and then I get to know people and I just can't be arsed following rules…Because it's shit…That's how I am. (Tom, 15)

A number of the young people spoke in an abstract way, of having made friends in care, but very few seemed to keep in touch. Others spoke of forming relationships which abruptly ended when they were moved to different placements leaving them with feelings of intense loss:

> I weren't 16, I didn't have a say in anything…They just dragged me away from everything. They just picked me up and took me away from everything I had. (John, 18)

The residential workers interviewed were keen to stress that the decision to close down a placement and move the young person on was not taken lightly. Two of the unit managers felt that it was more likely to occur if the young person had already experienced multiple placements prior to entering their establishments and displayed 'entrenched' patterns of behaviour, which were not amenable to change:

> Placement break downs here are quite rare, but that's not to say that we haven't had. And that's quite often been really when we've had young people who've had multiple placements, come here with a range of difficult behaviours, and we're just not successful in changing that. And then the impact on the other young people and on the service, generally. We then would have to make a decision with (the local authority) that this isn't, kind of, appropriate, and then we would need to look at alternatives. Quite often, that would be led by serious offences and police involvement. (Children's Home Manager)

> If you're admitting a youngster, you're taking on that commitment. I mean, it's happened at (the unit), when you get to a time when you think, 'We're certainly not doing this youngster any good. We're going to have to be looking at moving this youngster to another home'. And that doesn't happen overnight. It takes weeks to determine that. And once you make that decision, you're certainly not approaching the Authority and saying, 'We've closed this off today'. It doesn't happen like that, it can't. It's a big commitment you're taking on. (Children's Home Manager)

Here, the residential workers highlight a number of potential justifications for non-finance related placement moves, including the impact of challenging behaviour on other residents and the ability of the home to provide their contracted service (indeed homes are inspected and assessed on their ability to produce positive outcomes), along with the perceived 'risk' to the individual young person of remaining in a placement where his or her 'needs' are not being met. While these points certainly have a degree of validity and it is undoubtedly both difficult and stressful for workers and other residents to be faced with persistently challenging behaviour, it is nevertheless the case that multiple placement movement can have devastating effects upon a young person's short- and long-term behaviour, as well as further disrupting educational provision and it is surely incumbent upon those responsible for their care and welfare to ensure that it only occurs as a matter of last resort.

Along with the more immediate effects such as those experienced by Emma and John, Munro and Hardy (2007, p.3) highlight how 'young people experiencing high levels of placement instability have previously been found to have the poorest levels of adjustment in terms of employment, social relationships, financial management and housing (Biehal et al. 1995)'. Indeed, in the context of this study, it was often the case that a rootless, itinerant lifestyle remained a feature of the lives of the young people after they had left their respective children's homes. Some drifted between temporary semi-independent and/or hostel accommodation, the homes of partners with whom they had short-lived relationships, and prison sentences. For Peter, who continued to experience instability and, at the age of 17 had to leave the children's home where he had been resident for approximately 18 months after assaulting a local resident, this resulted in accommodation instability for some time:

> Stayed at Travel Lodge, which Social Services arranged. Then homeless for two days, stayed at mates for a month, then Action for Children found me a place...then have lived with some girl-friends. (Peter, 20)

Such instability frequently accompanied, and to a degree, seemed to perpetuate the continuation of an offending lifestyle by the young people. This may be linked to attachment theory (Hirschi, 1969, cited in Taylor, 2006), which posits that criminality is caused by the lack of strong, positive relationships, which cannot readily be formed if a person does not stay in one place for very long. Certainly, one residential worker commented upon the benefits of not giving up when a young person consistently displays difficult behaviour:

> A lot of them, when they come here, they'll try out things to see what our staying power is as well. Are we going to be there when they've done their worst? Are we going to be there to support them? So a lot of them will come in, and their behaviour will really be up the scale and then after about a year, even less than a year, it will come down and down and down, and that's because we sort of don't give up. (Residential Worker)

Here the value of 'not giving up' is clearly endorsed and can produce positive outcomes. In addition, it should not be forgotten that, as highlighted in the previous chapter, there is an acknowledged variability in the quality of residential children's homes across the public and private sectors, with certain regimes and methods of working with young people having been found to produce better outcomes than others (King, Raynes and Tizard, 1973; Whitaker, Archer and Hicks, 1998; Sinclair and Gibbs, 1998; Berridge and Brodie, 1998; Brown et al., 1998; Clough, 2000; Berridge, 2002; Anglin, 2002; Hicks et al., 2007; Kilpatrick et al., 2008; Kendrick, 2012). It is therefore important not to allow a risk-averse focus on the behaviour of individual young people to obscure the fact that part of the reason for such behaviour may lie in the nature of care provided. As will be discussed in the next section, this includes a paucity of provision designed to meet the needs of individual young people

Limitation and homogeneity of placements

> It seems as though they're slotted into places not suitable for the children, but suitable for the system. So they might be taken out of their neighbourhood or their family surroundings and moved wherever...That's our impression: that they need to fit into the system, not the system that's fitting them. (Magistrate)

Here, the magistrate reveals a commonly held perception amongst many of the youth justice professionals and indeed O'Neill (2008) highlights that one effect of the contraction of the residential sector is that there are fewer and less specialised children's homes, which limits the opportunity for matching children's needs with the most appropriate provision. Certainly, in Sarah's case, the manager of her former privately run residential unit expressed how, at times, they found it extremely difficult to deal with her behaviour:

> I felt out of my depth, as did the team, with Sarah...They were bandying about 'personality disorder'. I just felt ill-equipped...We've got this; this is what the health professionals say, where do we go now? (Children's Home Manager)

The home ultimately ended up involving the youth justice system, largely because they felt that there was little else they could do to tackle and control her challenging behaviour. The manager also spoke of the difficulties of accessing mental health services in respect of Sarah, a problem which was further compounded by the fact that she was placed out of her local authority area. Therefore, Sarah was further criminalised despite the failings of the home and social services, to adequately meet her needs. Such concerns were expressed by other professionals:

> In a perfect world, we'd love to have units that catered for every category of... young person, with every difficulty, and that's not going to happen. So, children tend to get thrown together in units that can't respond to every difficulty they have. (YOT Worker)

Given the emotional and behavioural difficulties presented by many young people entering residential child care (McCann et al., 1996; Berridge and Brodie, 1998; Meltzer et al., 2004) it is imperative that serious thought is given to how this situation might be improved, including a consideration of whether it might now be appropriate to expand residential sector provision and what form this should take. With an average of £3,860 per child per week being spent on private/voluntary provision (DfE, 2013a) and relatively inexpensive housing in some parts of northern England, it is unsurprising that companies have seized the opportunity to make up the shortfall in provision. However, there is always the risk that they will accept those for whom they are not equipped to provide an effective service (as was the case with Sarah) in order to maintain income generation and profitability. Such considerations have unfortunately been found to prevail with private provision in other sectors (Scourfield, 2007) and were a frequently voiced concern of a number of the professionals in this study. Thus far, while quality of care has been found to be variable across public and private placements (Berridge and Brodie, 1998; the research presented in this book), with recent Ofsted inspections finding no distinct difference between the performance of homes by sector (DfE, 2012a), it is clear that the 'generic' provision so prevalent across sectors undoubtedly falls short of meeting the needs of many young people, with only a limited number of specialised and often very expensive placements offering a more tailored service. A significant number of providers tend to adopt a 'we take all comers' approach (Rose, 2002, p.191) which can have unfortunate consequences for some.

Indeed, that such factors may have their part to play in the precipitation of offending is also evidenced by the comments made by some of the professionals concerning the prevalence of girls from children's homes who come through the courts:

There are as many girls as there are boys. (Magistrate)

Official statistics reveal that overall females are significantly less likely to come to the attention of the criminal justice system: 1,246,320 persons were convicted and sentenced at all courts in 2011 of which 24 per cent were female (MoJ, 2012), and females accounted for 22 per cent of the young people Youth Offending Teams reported working within 2010–2011 (YJB/MOJ, 2012). Nevertheless, in the context of this study, some of the professionals perceived that, in terms of young people from children's homes who appeared before the court, girls were as prevalent as boys. Such perceptions concur to a certain extent with the data obtained from the initial stages of this research, which, although obviously not statistically generalisable, identified a 50–50 gender split in the 18 children and young people in residential care who appeared in youth court during the 12 month period surveyed. However, between them, the nine boys appeared on many more occasions, accounting for 70 per cent of the total sentencing appearances of the sample, with the nine girls accounting for 30 per cent. This is still higher than the total number of young people who appeared for sentencing in Coalton Youth Court during that period, of which only 15 per cent were female.

This chimes with research from the USA which found that when compared to females in the general child and youth population, females within the child welfare system faced particularly high levels of risk for adolescent incarceration (Jonson-Reid and Barth, 2000). Taylor (2006) reveals how 'the authors note that this does not necessarily mean that child welfare services are causing poor outcomes for females: rather there are serious gaps in our understanding of how males and females differ in their responses to maltreatment and service experiences'. Nevertheless, O'Neill

(2008) reports how previous research has found that there are gender differences in the experience of living in residential care and, while outcomes for both boys and girls remain poor overall, there is evidence that they are worse for girls. O'Neill highlights how policy and practice in recent years has resulted in the majority of residential homes accommodating boys and girls together, although it has been shown that any benefits of this 'normalising' arrangement are predominantly benefits for boys, with girls' (who at approximately 37 per cent constitute the overall minority in children's homes, DfE, 2013) needs subordinated or unrecognised, even where they are the majority in homes (Berridge and Brodie 1998; Farmer and Pollock 1998, cited in O'Neill, 2008). It is concluded that :

> There has been little recognition that the needs of girls may be different from those of boys, or that alternative approaches and policies may be needed to respond to them. This has compounded the marginalisation of already socially excluded girls in institutional care, who are expected to 'fit into' provision primarily designed for boys, resulting in even worse outcomes for girls than for their male peers. (O'Neill, 2008, p.102)

This is potentially extremely damaging for young women, both in terms of their short and longer term outcomes, including involvement with the youth justice system, and is certainly an area which merits further research.

Size of placements

> Over time they funnel them into more individualised, private placements. We've had a few here. We've got the two-to-one ratio. And that's expensive, and sometimes you think...they're not getting any kind of normal lifestyle...They've got two adults sitting on them all day, all night. They take them out, do things with them, to vary it, but it becomes very claustrophobic for them...And they kick against it, 'Why can't I go down the street and make some friends, why can't I go into Coalton with some mates?' And so they do become very claustrophobic and paranoid, I've noticed. (Matthew, YOT)

As illustrated by the above quote, another identified source of conflict occurred when young people were moved on to single child units in order to attempt to curtail challenging behaviour. While some of the young people spoke of their preference for smaller units, for James, being in such a placement was a step too far:

> Couldn't cope with the place. Boring. Had to do education throughout the day and an activity at night. Can't do an activity with myself... Did my head in... I just flipped. (James, 16)

For James, the frustration that he felt as a result of being resident in a single child unit came to the fore when he committed a number of assaults and criminal damages against staff and property in the home. He also kept putting himself at risk by running away. These incidents were often reported to the police and resulted in court appearances, albeit on occasion, in conjunction with other, more serious offences. The author of one of his Pre-Sentence Reports, indicates that James had expressed unhappiness at being placed in a unit where there were no other young people, and that, on occasion, he felt that presenting challenging behaviour would speed up the process of getting a move. When being interviewed for this research, James described how he felt that larger, mixed gender units were preferable to single placement units, where he evidently did not enjoy being under such a level of scrutiny. Given that for many of the young people, peer associations became an important source of empowerment and self-worth, it was perhaps the case that to be isolated from other young people in such a way, cut James off from a valuable source of social recognition and made him feel estranged from 'normal' life. Indeed, Clough, Bullock and Ward (2006) argue that a small home denies the potential for residents to be supportive to others in groups, something which has been found to be important to young people (Emond, 2003), along with having others to share interests and activities with (Morgan, 2009).

Clough, Bullock and Ward (2006, p.61) further point out that the issue of the optimal size of a residential home is an important one, especially as the number of residents is dropping, to the point where residential units for two children or even one child are becoming common. Indeed, as of 31 March 2013, 101 (6 per cent) of the children's homes registered with Ofsted were for just one place, with a further 239 (14 per cent) registered for two places (DfE, 2013a). Although two influential studies (Sinclair and Gibbs, 1998; Berridge and Brodie, 1998) lead to a clear statement that on the whole, it is better to keep the size of children's homes small, Clough, Bullock and Ward argue that:

> Very small residential homes are extremely costly to staff and seem to emulate some of the characteristics of a foster home without the key factors that make a foster home akin to a family setting: the fact that foster parents share the home with the child and do not go on and off duty. In small homes each child has far greater potential to disrupt the stability of life in the residential home, and produce a situation in which much of what happens is a direct response to his or her own behaviour. (2006, p.61)

Of course, such factors must be balanced against findings high-lighted in the previous chapter regarding the potential for negative peer cultures, bullying and violence (Polsky, 1962; Taylor, 2006; Barter, 2008; Barter et al., 2004; Sinclair and Gibbs, 1998) and the question to consider therefore seems to be how we can preserve and enhance the positive aspects of peer relationships, whilst ensuring that the more undesirable elements are curtailed.

With regard to smaller homes more generally, opinions amongst the young people were mixed. Some could appreciate their advantages in terms of the increased staff attention they received and being less frenetic places to live, while at the same time feeling that there was more 'atmosphere' in the larger units. In the Coalton area, a retrenchment of residential provision had taken place in the 18 months prior to the commencement of the research study, with the closure of two larger residential homes and their replacement with two smaller units accommodating approximately 5–6 young people. Those who could not be accommodated in the newer units were dispersed to other sometimes 'out of area' placements. The former larger residential homes had a bad reputation locally, with their residents often viewed as being out of control and criminally inclined. Indeed, a number of the professionals commented upon this and felt that the new smaller units had improved the quality of care provided, and outcomes for the young people. Nevertheless, the proposition that a smaller placement does not necessarily result in a higher quality of care and can, at times, perpetuate difficulties, is further reinforced by comments made by other professionals, which indicate that the culture of individual homes and associated staff-resident interactions, including their ability to respond to individual needs are as crucial as ever in terms of outcomes, regardless of size:

> One of the girls I dealt with latterly, it was a single placement. She was the only child and needed the whole staff group around her, and I think there were as many inconsistencies there, really…very difficult. (YOT Worker)

> With the smaller numbers, units are more able to…deal with difficulties. That isn't to say they don't arise with the more complex cases. They do, and it seems to me at times that staff are still a little bit adrift as to what to do with those presenting problems. I think they still struggle with that. (YOT Worker)

Indeed, recent Ofsted inspections (DfE, 2013a) found that there was no statistically significant correlation between overall effectiveness and the size of homes, which appears to add additional weight to the contention that smaller units in and of themselves will not necessarily produce better outcomes in terms of addressing offending and challenging behaviour unless other vital elements are in place. These include a staff group who are equipped to deal with the presenting issues and a positive, consistent culture (Whitaker, Archer and Hicks, 1998; Sinclair and Gibbs, 1998; Berridge and Brodie, 1998; Brown et al., 1998; Hicks et al., 2007; Anglin, 2002). Sometimes, the impression was conveyed that single placement homes in particular were merely exercises in containment for children deemed to be extremely challenging, a concept which could just as easily be applied to the next theme.

Isolated placements

John described how, in response to his behaviour, he was placed in various 'isolated' placements:

> When I got moved to 'The Manor', that was the first isolated unit they put me in. It was on the moors. If you tried to leave, they

phoned the police. You couldn't leave; you had to be with staff all the time. I lived there about six-months. It went alright. I did good there, so they let me move on. They put me in a proper home after that. And then I got bad again, so they put me in 'Buttercup Place'. And that's isolated and it's horrible, as well. It's in the middle of nowhere. It's freezing, snow six-foot deep all the time. (John, 18)

For John, being placed in such units caused him considerable frustration which resulted in further offending:

Social Services think that by putting you in an isolated unit that you'll change, but it just makes you worse... All your anger builds up. Like when I lived in 'Buttercup Place', I've never done more criminal damage in my life. Because you couldn't go out anywhere. If you were angry, you couldn't go off the unit, you had to stay with staff or you were reported missing... You had to be within sight, where you could be seen, but that was well depressing. If you was pissed off about something, and you couldn't even have your own space. So, by putting me there, it just made me worse. I stole a car; that was the first time I'd ever stolen a car... I just wanted to get away from there. (John, 18)

Such placements seem to be very near embodiments of Goffman's 'total institution' where young people are sent in an effort to make them conform and change their behaviour. John describes receiving educational input at the units, and there were activities that could be undertaken in the evenings, sometimes off-site. From a Foucauldian perspective, such units could be said to be encompass the attributes of a 'complete institution', employing techniques of hierarchical observation, normalising judgement and examination. However, resistance to the power of the institution can be found in John's attempts to 'escape' and the other offences of criminal damage. It is unclear from John's account whether his placements were officially designated secure children's homes, although they seem to be similar in substance to Approved Schools where offenders were sent in the 1950s and 1960s. Such placements are reminiscent of an earlier philosophy of removing children and young people from their immediate environments and the perceived negative influence of other people, in the hope that this would lead to a change in behaviour, thus focusing upon the reformation of the 'aberrant individual', to the exclusion of wider contributory factors. Indeed, Frost, Mills and Stein describe how, in 1609, another major idea of child welfare emerged-the idea of migration to the colonies:

> Primary amongst the ideas which influenced the policy was that children can be reformed by the countryside and the fresh air, that indigenous poverty can be 'solved' by such solutions, and that children had a better chance of success if separated from the environment, and the people, including their parents, who had contributed to their 'downfall'. (1999, p.12)

It appears that such ideas are resonant today and it might be the case that certain young people can benefit from such a placement. However, for John it engendered feelings of loneliness, isolation and separation from all with which he was familiar, thus precipitating further offending. In addition to the potential disadvantages of such a placement, John also described how he was not visited by a social services representative for several months, after his social worker had a car accident, which meant that he could not voice his unhappiness with the placement. The impression is therefore conveyed that he was simply left there, 'out of sight, out of mind':

> She lied to me as well... I'm going there for two months, she said. And then I didn't see her for seven months. She should have come for a meeting, but she cancelled it because she had a car accident. And then three months later, she only just came out. This is what I mean. I wanted to move, but I couldn't tell her, because she didn't come to see me. (John, 18)

The difficulty of visiting distant placements was mentioned by one of the field social workers, who commented that due to the contraction in local authority provision, this was becoming more of an issue. Sinclair and Gibbs (1998) found that residents of private homes had less frequent contact with their families and were much less well informed about the plans for their future (e.g. about where they would go and when) and less likely to be happy about those plans. Both as a result of the lack of provision in their local areas and their 'challenging' behaviour, many of the young people in this study were eventually placed in 'out of authority', private placements. Tickle (2012) highlights how it has long been accepted that – safeguarding factors aside – it is better for children in care to live close to home. However, the most recently available statistics show that 46 per cent of young people in children's homes were placed outside their local authority boundary (DfE, 2013a) and in 2011 the then children's minister Tim Loughton felt it necessary to send a letter reminding councils of the need to reduce the number of out-of-area placements being made. Several of the young people in this study described finding it hard to settle and placing themselves at risk by running away in order to return to family and friends, when they were placed in different areas:

> I didn't like it. It were too far away from home … I kept running off and going to my mates and stuff … Because me mates were so far away from me, I just wanted to be with them. (Lucy, 17)

> If they put me somewhere else, then I'd run away, back to where my family was. (Robbie, 17)

This is in accordance with previous research which found that being unhappy and missing family were reasons why children and young people go missing from care (Morgan, 2006). It is also the case that distance between the child and their family may limit and undermine the scope for work with the whole family, as well as curtailing social work contact and oversight.

Not being heard

Not being listened to regarding unhappiness with a placement was also cited as a reason for going missing from care (Morgan, 2006) and indeed, as expressed by Robbie, such experiences were often linked to a feeling on the part of the young people that their wishes were disregarded:

> Every time they put me somewhere … it was away from my family. I didn't want to be there … I didn't have the choice of coming back, it was out of my hands, and that frustrated me and made me angry. (Robbie, 17)

Certainly such experiences are hardly conducive to a young person accepting and being able to settle into a children's home and are reflective of similar perceptions reported by the Children's Rights Director (Morgan, 2011), who found that only 50 per cent of the 179 children in care who were consulted, felt their social worker or caseworker took notice of their wishes and feelings with regard to the decisions made about their care. Of course, the legislative right to be consulted does not necessarily equate to a child or young person's opinion being given precedence when the final decision is made and there may be a number of reasons for this, including the need to take account of safeguarding factors. However, a lack of regard for a child's wishes could also relate to adults presuming to know what is best in such situations in accordance with concomitant discourses relating both to the superiority of adult judgement and perceptions of children as 'potential persons' in need of guidance (Fawcett, Featherstone and Goddard, 2004). Indeed, in terms of the right to participation in decision making, Emond (2008, p.188) argues that:

> This aspect of the children's rights movement is underpinned by the notion that children's opinions and wishes are worth knowing. This in itself is quite a recent and not homogeneously held belief.

Certainly, with regard to children in care who so often are perceived as either 'victims' or 'villains', it could well be that professionals fail to give adequate weight to their wishes. In addition, the interplay of power relations is again evidenced by a comment made by one of the social workers concerning the decision not to readily acquiesce to James's desire to be moved to a placement nearer his family:

> He was saying he wanted to come back. We were saying we didn't want to bring him back immediately, because that was, like, rewarding his behaviour. (Social Worker)

The decision to keep James at a particular placement therefore appeared to be designed to send a message both to the individual young person and others in the system, that the institution and the system was in charge, and that a lack of co-operation would not be tolerated (Goffman, 1961).

Nevertheless, professionals are themselves subject to a number of constraints which may impede their ability to respond to children's individual preferences, regardless of what their professional values might suggest and incline them towards. The issue of financial constraints and the lack of availability of local placements inherent in the contraction of the residential sector have already been discussed and indeed, Bell (2002, p.2) argues that, 'the dominant value base of Social Service Departments today is business efficiency rather than the human rights of children'. With regard to often extremely vulnerable young people, such pre-occupations could result in them exercising their resistance to decisions which have been made on their behalf and without their agreement by either displaying challenging behaviour or placing themselves in further danger by running away.

Conclusion

It is undeniable that the overarching policy and system arrangements relating to the English care system clearly have a profound impact upon the experiences of the young people and their potential to come to the attention of the youth justice system. Placement movement for financial/strategic reasons, as well as in 'risk-averse' response to troublesome behaviour can result in further emotional and psychological damage to already vulnerable individuals, thus perpetuating additional challenging behaviour and damaging long-term effects. Here, the value of 'not giving up' is clearly resonant. In addition, a lack of placement choices means that young people often cannot be matched to provision which would best suit their needs, with many providers adopting a 'we take all comers' (Rose, 2002, p.191) approach that can at times result in them being unable to deal with presenting issues; consequently seeking recourse to the youth justice system or closing down the placement meaning that the young person has to move again. Girls in particular may be adversely affected by such a strategy. Moreover, issues relating to the ever-decreasing size of placements, isolated placements and the perception of many young people that their feelings and wishes are not taken into account particularly when they were placed in areas away from family and friends, have the potential to further contribute to conflict and negative outcomes. Certainly, while many young people enter residential care with presenting problems, it is clear that their experiences of care system policy and practice can both exacerbate existing problems and create new ones and that as a consequence, fresh thought needs to be given to the nature of available provision and the value of giving real consideration to young people's individual needs and preferences in accordance with the spirit of existing legislation, rather than responding to them as an homogenous group in need of containment and control.

7
'Policing', Power and Perceptions

They always called the police. Even if it's small, pointless, in your bedroom, they always called the police. In Coalton, they were always getting you arrested. It's like they don't want you to be there. (Robbie, 17)

There was an argument over the phone. The care-worker had hold of the phone, saying, 'You can't use it.' The lad had hold of the wire, tugging on the wire and the wire snapped, and they phoned the police, and he gets charged with criminal damage. (Solicitor)

She kicks off because she doesn't want to get up at nine in the morning... throws a cushion at member of staff, and then pushes member of staff, no injuries sustained, and she's into court for assault. (YOT Worker)

Each home has got their own rules and regulations about 'policing' they call it... 'You'll be policed.' I've heard that a lot. (Police Officer)

Introduction

The following chapter will explore a number of important questions surrounding the management of residential home based challenging behaviour, an issue which has been consistently highlighted as being a significant contributory factor in the criminalisation of young people in children's homes (Nacro, 2012, 2005, 2003; Morgan, 2006; Taylor, 2006; Fitzpatrick, 2009; Darker, Ward and Caulfield, 2008), with a particularly low threshold reported for police involvement. As illustrated by Robbie's account (see above) this was confirmed by many of the young people in this study and highlighted by a number of the youth justice professionals as being an issue of particular concern to them. The chapter will then proceed to explore how the young people are viewed by the youth court when prosecuted for children's home based incidents, including how care status might potentially impact upon their experiences and subsequent outcomes.

The 'policing' and prosecution of residential home based 'offences'

Chapter 1 describes in some detail how, at the time of writing, attempts to address the issues surrounding the unnecessary criminalisation of children's home residents include the use of formal practice protocols developed in consultation with various agencies, including the police, Youth Offending Teams and residential children's home providers. Such protocols have the aim of managing behaviour within children's homes, while avoiding recourse to the youth justice system wherever possible, and are often used in tandem with 'in-house' restorative justice techniques (see Willmott, 2007; Littlechild and Sender, 2010).

Nevertheless, police involvement for minor matters remains a persistent problem, with Schofield et al. (2012) reporting that while there are excellent examples of practice at a local level, policy commitments and practice protocols to prevent unnecessary criminalisation are 'not working well enough' (ibid., p.5). Indeed, as Hayden (2010, p.12) points out the devil is often in the detail, with the successful implementation of a particular protocol often dependent on whether individuals have 'read it, understood it, supported its values and purpose and then knew how to use it in their response'. Certainly, in Coalton, a formal protocol had been in place for approximately 18 months, yet both the young people and professionals reported a continuation of youth justice involvement for minor matters, albeit at a reduced rate. This strongly suggests that decisions to involve the police are in part due to the presence of factors which have so far proved impervious to the presence of formal guidance. This chapter will therefore explore the attitudes and perceptions of those professionals who are directly responsible for the care and control of the young people with a view to considering how these might impact upon their thinking and subsequent responses to challenging behaviour.

Contrasting professional perspectives

When questioned about their dealings with young people in residential care, the youth justice professionals were mainly of the view that they were unnecessarily criminalised for minor matters that would not have been brought to the attention of the police had they taken place within the family home:

> I do think it's a shame that a lot of children in care come to court for silly reasons. They've damaged a light bulb or they've damaged a cupboard door ... Or they've hit out at the carers perhaps ... I think it should be dealt with in the home, not in court ... Because you put them on the ladder of the criminal justice system ... I think the court is not the place to address it. (Magistrate)

Indeed, a number of the magistrates expressed a perception that young people in residential care mainly appear for minor matters, with the more serious cases usually involving those who still live with their families. This perhaps highlights how the residential care experience can be 'protective' in some respects, but precipitant and damaging in others. Nevertheless, the contrast between their perceptions and those of the social services and care system professionals is particularly striking. Indeed, the social workers conveyed the impression that more often than not the police were justifiably called, by well-meaning staff, to deal with extremely challenging young people as a last resort, because there was nothing else that could be done to contain their behaviour:

> She just pushed and pushed and pushed, and it was the last resort of the residential home to say: 'We can't do any more; we need to phone the police.' (Social Worker)

It was assumed that as a result of the nature and disposition of the young people, residential care staff had no choice but to inform the authorities, even in instances where the resident had little or no youth justice involvement prior to entering care. Such attitudes have worrying implications both in terms of their propensity to view the young people as a homogenous group in need of containment and control (see also Chapter 4) and the lack of consideration of the impact of involvement with the youth justice system and the consequent acquisition of a criminal record.

Frequency of incidents

Residential home staff and managers were generally keen to stress that the police were usually only called as a last resort:

> The policy is that you call the police as a last resort…I guess crucially, it's when there is a real, genuine, risk to staff or service users, or to the young person themselves. So (the decision to call the police) is not taken lightly at all…we have sustained significant damage to the property and not called the police. (Residential Care Worker)

However, despite the above comment, which implied that the primary criteria for police involvement was the perceived level of threat involved in an incident, many others conveyed the impression that it was the frequency, rather than the particular seriousness of incidents, that appeared to be most pertinent. Indeed, the incidents previously alluded to give a flavour of the relatively petty nature of some of the reported 'offences'. Nevertheless, it was apparent that the residential staff felt that police involvement was necessary as the ultimate sanction, when all other options had failed:

> It's not a routine response. It's a considered response. If that behaviour is prevalent…it's all about trying to turn that youngster's behaviour to something more appropriate…If you've exhausted all your care practices within the home, then yeah, it's the right thing to do. (Children's Home Manager)

Indeed, some expressed the view that police involvement could serve as a 'wake-up call' to the 'realities' of life, which many perceived the young people to be sometimes estranged or unhelpfully protected from, in the residential context:

Occasionally, if it's on-going... It may be that we then call in the police, because there's a way of making them realise that this is the reality of what life's about. (Residential Worker)

Once it goes on and on and on and on, there has to be a cut-off point where you're showing the child the consequences of their actions and if they lived out in the real world, when they get out of care, they can't carry on like that, and they will be arrested if they cause damage to anybody else's property. (Police Officer)

The fact that in the 'real world', it would not in all likelihood occur to a child's parents to involve the police for minor matters of criminal damage committed within the family home and that there might be numerous pre- and in-care factors which have contributed to such behaviour does not seem to be at the forefront of considerations; indeed these comments are further evidence of the dominance of the discourse of individualisation of 'offending' and the idea that children and young people should be made 'to face up to' and 'take responsibility' for their actions.

Maintaining the authority of staff and unit

Nevertheless, as with previous research (TACT, 2008), comments made by two of the professionals suggested that the 'moral guidance' of individual children and young people might not always be uppermost in the minds of staff. Rather, the need to preserve the overall authority of staff and the unit, and send out a warning to other residents regarding the consequences of misbehaviour, could also be pertinent factors:

I think that it's sort of a lesson that they're trying to teach the other young people... That this is your home, and while you're living here, you're here to look after it, and if you do damage it, you will be punished. (Leaving Care Worker)

Indeed a further indication of the need to maintain the overall authority of the home could be found when staff and managers talked about different levels of misdemeanour. While most were keen to stress that property damage would often be initially tolerated, as with previous research (Hayden, 2010), it was indicated that 'violence' directed towards staff would not:

> If a staff member has been assaulted, then I would definitely support the staff (in involving the police). We shouldn't be coming to work and being assaulted. (Children's Home Manager)

> That would be at the staff's discretion, obviously. If they just slapped them, they might say, 'Don't do it next time'...It would be the degree of assault. But it would be down to the individual staff member as well. I would support my staff one hundred per cent. Whatever they decide, I'd go with. Because, at the end of the day, I'm there to support them, as well. (Children's Home Manager)

While staff safety is undeniably important, this policy seems to be more concerned with placating workers who might otherwise feel undermined: a display of staff solidarity intended to preserve the overall authority of the home, rather than considering the best interests of the young people by determining objectively whether an incident merits official intervention. Indeed, such comments raise important questions both regarding what should constitute an assault worthy of police involvement and the arbitrary nature of responses towards the young people.

The practice protocol in the case-study area contained a sliding-scale of offences and suggested methods of intervention, including when police involvement might be appropriate, with assaults being considered particularly serious. Nevertheless, instances of 'assaults' on staff where the police were called ranged from a worker being pushed out of the way when a young person was trying to leave a room after an argument, to a care worker having his nose broken. Certainly, if the decision to press charges is at the discretion of each individual staff member, this will inevitably produce an inconsistency in response, as some workers have a greater tolerance of such incidents than others. Undoubtedly, the same will also apply to instances of conflict between residents, such as those highlighted in Chapter 5. Here, an incident which might be treated as a relatively harmless fight between siblings in a family home and responded to via informal disciplinary measures could be brought to the attention of the police at the discretion of individual young people who are not otherwise constrained by the bonds of family loyalty. Such considerations point to the need to bring a degree of objectivity to the process of police involvement in assault cases, in terms of deciding whether official intervention is truly appropriate or whether the matter should be dealt with internally via other means.

Perceptions of powerlessness

The need to display solidarity amongst staff is perhaps also indicative of an overall sense of powerlessness, which is reflected in the perception that they are unable to deal 'effectively' with behavioural issues. Indeed, a residential unit manager expressed the view that police involvement was often necessary, due to the limited internal sanctions at their disposal:

> We clearly do not want to get people involved in the criminal justice system if at all possible. Then we also have to balance that with the limited consequences that we can use at the (home). Which in terms of sanctions, are limited, really ... I guess we're not able to do certain things that perhaps an ordinary parent would be able to do. (Children's Home Manager)

Exactly what the manager had in mind here was not clear in terms of how he envisaged an 'ordinary' parent being able to respond when their children misbehave. Nevertheless, his words reflected a commonly held view amongst all the professionals that an inability on the part of the homes and staff members to adequately monitor and control residents, contributed to offending:

> They don't have any teeth. They're limited in what they can do and what they can't do. (Social Worker)

Indeed, a frequently voiced concern was that residential workers were prevented from exercising 'appropriate' control and discipline, due to a fear of being made the subject of allegations of abuse by the young people, which could, potentially result in the loss of their job and criminal conviction. The image of the 'streetwise' child 'calling the shots' was pervasive:

The child calls the shots...they know exactly what their rights are with regard to being touched...so staff I think don't bother, because it's not worth it. It's not worth the complaint. (Police Officer)

Linked to this, was the notion on the part of some, that the situation had been worsened by the advent of legislation which conferred 'rights' upon the children and young people:

The Children Act...they all know what it is. 'You're touching me, you're not supposed to touch me.' do you know what I mean? So, you've just got to be careful all the time...How they get to know these rules and regulations just baffles me. They'll quote the rules and regulations, 'You can't do this, and you can't do that. You're not allowed to do that. I'll get my solicitor.' (Leaving Care Worker)

Such concerns are far from new: Emond (2008, p.183) suggests that it may be argued that viewing children as having social and legal rights has sparked greater debate and frustration amongst adults than it has amongst children – even more so amongst those working with children in public care. Indeed, in relation to the Children Act 1989, Utting (1997, p.109) asserts that, 'mention of children's rights provokes a sour response in some quarters, along the lines that the Children Act destroyed parental authority to control and discipline children'. Utting argues that underlying the Children Act, is a strong sense of the value of children, and that one of its main purposes is to safeguard and promote their welfare, including the right not to be physically or sexually abused. However, while pointing out that such rights are and remain important,

Around them, however, have grown myths of child dominance and omnipotence...The Children Act does not say that children must always have their own way, or that they must always be believed. Such loose attributions are made by adults grasping for excuses for welshing on their responsibilities to children. (Utting, 1997, p.109)

Nonetheless, such attributions are the very real and long-standing perceptions of a number of professionals. In 1998 Berridge and

Brodie (p.134) reported that in their attempts to explain serious behavioural problems, staff often referred to the issue of children's rights and children 'knowing too much'. It was felt that children had been empowered at the expense of staff, and that staff were consequently unable to deal effectively with behavioural issues. Certainly, this feeling was also prevalent amongst many of those that were interviewed in the present study, and indeed Smith (2009a, p.11) offers another perspective when arguing that statements of rights in their current superficial form are often more about protecting agencies from liability and can actually 'get in the way of healthy and just ways of negotiating differences and resolving conflicts, which should happen within the context of daily living and caring relationships', thus acting to 'build barriers between children and those who care for them'.

All the same, it is important that the adults responsible for their care give full and frank consideration to how their own behaviour and/or lack of a productive relationship with the young people might contribute to poor outcomes. As discussed previously, authoritarian regimes which expect young people to 'toe the line' and fail to respect them as individuals, have been found to produce poor outcomes and challenging behaviour. However, it also stands to reason that staff members who feel disempowered will be less likely to listen to and respect young people (Smith, 2009a) and be more likely to seek to manage challenging behaviour via the youth justice system. Nevertheless, it is apparent that where staff disempowerment occurs, its causes are multifarious, encompassing far more than the contested issue of children's statements of rights. Workers are often relatively poorly paid with many lacking qualifications and appropriate training in how to work with often very vulnerable, damaged and challenging young people (Colton and Roberts, 2007), and while Sinclair and Gibbs (1998) could find no evidence that either better-qualified staff (or a higher ratio of staff to children) predicted better outcomes, 'it is clear that the staff world is a very important factor in successful work' (Clough, Bullock and Ward, 2006, p.48). It has been suggested that:

It may be that there is a certain level of training that is essential for good outcomes or that some other staff factors such as confidence, morale, culture and leadership are more influential than training.

The conclusion seems to be that training is necessary but not, on its own, a sufficient condition for good practice. (ibid.)

Certainly, when contrasting children's residential care workers in the United Kingdom with the highly educated, high status, influential social pedagogues of northern Europe, Berridge et al. argue that:

In contrast, in children's residential care, their English equivalents have low status and little influence. Their professional input is marginalised and they lack autonomy. They usually refer on to experts rather than take control of issues themselves... our child care system is over-bureaucratic and risk averse. (2011, p.252)

This is once again connected to the 'last resort' status of residential care in the United Kingdom, which, as Berridge and Brodie (1998, p.10) point out, 'has continued to be seen as the poor relation of social work' and, as such, clearly has the potential to impact negatively upon outcomes. Linked to this, Clough, Bullock and Ward (2006) argue consideration should be given to whether available vocational and social work qualification based training courses may not be appropriate to the task of working in residential homes, something which will be further explored in the final chapter.

Police presence in children's homes

What is clear is that in the absence of staff empowerment, coupled with perceptions concerning the nature and characteristics of the young people, the value of police contact was emphatically endorsed by many. This included the focus group of residential care workers (RW), when they described how local police officers often visited their unit:

Researcher: Do the police have a regular presence in the home?

RW 1: A regular, positive presence. (A number of workers say 'yes' at this point). Especially the Police and Community Support Officer's and the community police officer... he comes once a month...

RW 2: For dinner!

RW 3: They'll just pop in to make sure that everything is alright...

RW 1: It's just to show them that they aren't just there to arrest them. Then they actually confront those issues at the table, as well.

RW 4: I think it also helps the police when they do have to come to an incident with our young people, that they've got an understanding of who our young people are, and their backgrounds.

RW 1: And they're not just carting them off and dealing with them. They kind of put the onus back on us to deal with things in-house, don't they? That's more positive than being arrested.

RW 5: I think that at times, if you can sense that something's brewing, you might ring the Police Community Support Officer's and see if they are in the area and see if they can pass by before it escalates, really.

Such sentiments were echoed by staff from the other homes:

We are very fortunate. We've got the local neighbourhood policeman and he's here nearly every day. It's a wonder he's not here now! He just comes and has a chat to us and the kids know him and I think that that's really good. (Children's Home Manager)

Positive aspects of such contact appear to include a greater understanding by the police of the young people's backgrounds and circumstances (something which was commented upon by the residential staff and confirmed by the police officers interviewed) and possible encouragement of staff by the police to deal with challenging behaviour 'in-house'. The potential also exists to open up lines of communication with the young people regarding matters of concern to them and related safeguarding issues. This is of particular importance in the wake of both historical cases of institutional abuse and the more recently highlighted propensity of certain individuals and groups within the community to target vulnerable young people for exploitation, as evidenced by the 2012 sex-trafficking convictions of a gang of men in Rochdale.

A primary aim of the police service youth strategy, 'It's Never Too Early... It's Never Too Late' (Carter, 2007), which was implemented on 24.1.08, is to build and maintain positive relationships between all young people and the police. The strategy document states that positive engagement with the police and their local communities will help to identify and support those children and young people who are at risk, and help all children and young people to enjoy a positive role within their communities. It is also stated that the police should aim to take a lead in identifying and diverting those children and young people at greatest risk of becoming involved in anti-social behaviour or criminality, before they enter the criminal justice system and before they are socially excluded. Various schemes which encourage police contact with children and young people in residential care have been implemented throughout the UK, and seem to be increasing in popularity. At the same time the *Children Act 1989 Guidance and Regulations Volume 5: Children's Homes* (DfE, 2013b) highlights how standard 3.22 requires that children's homes develop constructive relationships with police in their area (2.85). However, the incongruity of having a routine police presence in the homes of the young people was not lost on one of the professionals:

> Can you imagine that in your own house, police popping round for a coffee?! (Leaving Care worker)

Indeed, from another perspective, this practice could be said to be an extension of the surveillance and 'discipline' (Foucault, 1977) so prevalent within the institutional context and, as suggested by the focus group feedback, be primarily viewed by staff as a much needed way of 'keeping order'; the ultimate 'coercive back-up'. While such a practice might prove to have some value in terms of protecting certain young people, it could also be seen to carry with it an implicit presumption that the residents of such units are potential criminals, who should be treated accordingly and furthermore, serve to bring young people into contact with the police who might otherwise have had none. In a 'normal' home, a police presence would be viewed as an attack upon personal freedoms and civil liberties, as well as the integrity of the 'traditional' family unit. However, children in official institutions, adrift from the assumed regulation and discipline of the 'conventional' family structure, seem to be accorded no such respect. Little or no consideration appears to have been given to how this might impact upon the young people's often already negative self-image and consequent actions; the idea inherent in labelling theory (Lemert, 1967) that social control 'plays an active and propelling role in the creation and promotion of deviance' (Muncie, 2004, p.117) appears to have a particular resonance here, as do Foucault's ideas of how individual's in particular social settings and contexts are affected by power relations in terms of their self-identities, attitudes and their (psychological) predispositions.

Thought should also be given to the message this sends out to society at large about the nature of young people in residential care and its consequent implications. Taylor (2006, p.26) writes that 'popular perceptions continually link children in care with trouble', and indeed the 1992 Warner report found that, 'Children's homes are strongly associated in the public mind with deprived and delinquent children. Dickensian images of 19th century orphanages still linger on' (p.11). As discussed in Chapter 4, perceptions of young people in care as being either victims or villains has the potential to impact upon responses both from those who work directly with them and wider society, thus representing 'fundamental barriers to improving experiences of public care' (Taylor, 2006). It is therefore arguable that a routine and often very visible police presence in children's homes will serve to perpetuate such misapprehensions and might consequently do more harm than good. Careful thought should be given to whether this is truly appropriate and if the perceived benefits of such schemes could be achieved via other means. Certainly, it is arguable that if both staff and young people felt more empowered in the context of high quality residential provision, such intervention would be largely unnecessary.

The decision to prosecute

As will be illustrated in the following section, imprisonment could well be the outcome of a series of court appearances by a young person in residential care, thus making it particularly important to not only consider whether the police should be called in the first place, but also if decisions to prosecute reported incidents are sound. Current CPS legal guidance (www.cps.gov.uk) states that:

> The police are more likely to be called to a children's home than a domestic setting to deal with an incident of offending behaviour by an adolescent. Specialists should bear this in mind when

dealing with incidents that take place in a children's home....A criminal justice disposal...should not be regarded as an automatic response to offending behaviour by a looked after child, irrespective of their criminal history.

In an attempt to address the issue, the Coalton Crown Prosecution Service youth specialist prosecutor had recently taken the step of ensuring that in cases involving young people from residential children's homes, contact was made with the home to find out what steps had been put in place to discipline the young person before they decided to involve the police, in order to guard against 'inappropriate' prosecutions. Nevertheless, while this might go some way towards achieving the aim of making homes think twice about involving the police, it could also be argued that if a home reports that they have tried their best over a period of time with a 'difficult' young person, then this is unlikely to make a great deal of difference. Indeed, one children's home manager described how they had recently started to compile a dossier of incidents at the home involving each young person, which was taken to court hearings, in order to prove that a number of incidents had taken place before the police were called. This, in turn, might serve to create an even worse impression of the young person for the court, having been presented with a list of their misdemeanours. Again, it is arguable that in respect of children in residential care, the focus should be upon whether each individual incident merits police involvement and prosecution rather than considering cumulative behaviour.

The youth court: sentencing issues

The Magistrates Association Youth Courts Committee recently expressed that magistrates were 'extremely concerned' about children in care being brought to court for offences which would 'certainly not reach court if the children lived in conventional families' (2012, p.4) and indeed, in the context of this research, many expressed their frustration at having to deal with 'petty' incidents regarding children's home residents, especially when the same young people kept being returned to court:

Honestly, you sit in the retiring room and you think, 'What can we do with this case?' (Magistrate)

> We go in the back to discuss it, and it's very frustrating... All you can do is the best that you can come up with on that particular day, and hope it works. (Magistrate)

> Inevitably, they do tend to move up the scale... As they build up a long record, you have to say, 'We've tried everything', and they end up with a Detention and Training Order. (Magistrate)

The potentially negative impact of numerous court appearances in terms of defendants moving up the sentencing tariff as the result of a series of relatively minor incidents to imprisonment was a concern expressed by a number of the youth justice professionals, and seemed to be borne out by the experiences of many of the young people in this study.

Impact of care status and carers reports

It was also suggested that a young person's care status might in itself negatively impact upon the way their behaviour is perceived and consequently dealt with by the court:

> It can be regarded as simply as naughty behaviour by children who ought to be behaving better. I think sometimes benches have some 1950's, 1960's view of kids, who ought to line up for their meals, be grateful for three bowls of gruel a day. With some Benches, with some personalities, there's an element of that. (YOT Worker)

Similarly, a solicitor commented that an 'assault' committed on a care home staff member might be viewed more seriously:

> I think the courts tend to regard that as more serious than a run of the mill assault... because it was a person in the home who was in a position of authority. (Solicitor)

Although this possibility was only mentioned on two occasions, it is certainly something that I experienced during my relatively recent time as a court officer with a Youth Offending Team, and is further evidenced by the reasoning given by magistrates for the imposition of a six-month custodial sentence upon a 15-year-old girl, Jasmine. Jasmine's Pre-Sentence Report revealed that she had numerous convictions for common assault, all committed against staff in residential settings, after being received into care following a particularly traumatic early childhood. The reasons given for the Detention and Training Order were stated as follows:

> You are again before the court for assault and threatening behaviour committed against people who are trying to help you ... we have heard about an awful series of incidents where people were afraid for the personal safety of your supervisor ... who was doing her job and doing everything she possibly could do to help you. We have perused your appalling record for violence and no sentence imposed by the courts has prevented you from re-offending. We do not accept that you are genuinely remorseful. (Memorandum of an entry entered in the Register of Coalton Youth Court for 14.6.07)

It is therefore entirely possible that the perceived ingratitude of a child in care, along with a desire to assist 'beleaguered' staff, could be a motivating factor in sentencing decisions. Perhaps predictably, it was something which no magistrate interviewed during the course of this research was prepared to volunteer as a specific reason. Indeed, all six were keen to stress that, if anything, the young person was given more leeway than otherwise might have been the case, due to their care status, a perception which was echoed by other professionals:

> I think if they were from a different circumstance or from a different background, I think they'd be given a whole lot less leeway ... I think, because of their background ... they are a lot more, sort of, 'We'll give you another chance.' (Residential Care Worker)

> I always thought that with Sam, you could have a bit of leeway, because you could go in and tug on the heart strings a bit ... You do maybe use some of the facts of their background as a bit of a ... you present them in a way that you try and get the old sympathy vote. (YOT Worker)

While this may have an element of truth, it stands to reason that reports of a general, on-going lack of co-operation within the home by the young person, might impact negatively upon the courts view of that individual and consequently, its sentencing decision. After all, dominant discourse indicates that while parents are held responsible for their children's behaviour and seen as having failed if it does not come up to 'acceptable' standards, care workers are often viewed as being in semi-official positions, trying to do their best with 'difficult' young people. Indeed, some magistrates expressed how reports from carers could, potentially, impact upon sentencing decisions:

> It is helpful to have a carer there to give you the picture of what that child's like in the home. Whether they're helpful and pleasant and have friends or whether they are always argumentative. (Magistrate)

Such comments reveal a naiveté and lack of understanding regarding how the often negative pre- and in-care experiences of the young people impact upon their subsequent behaviour in the residential context. Indeed, a teenager residing in a 'normal' family home might struggle to live up to such standards and it is arguable that expecting a young person who will in all likelihood have experienced pre-care abuse and/or neglect, along with a whole range of turbulent in-care experiences, to be consistently helpful and pleasant is completely unrealistic.

As illustrated by the following quotes, it could also be argued that to assume care-workers or other professionals are completely neutral in their assessments of the young people and uninfluenced by other considerations, is somewhat unrealistic:

> You do get some adults who think that kids should be just appreciative that they're being looked after; that there's somebody prepared to do that. They're the people I worry about. (Residential Unit Manager)
>
> I think sometimes social services...would be quite pleased if the young person got locked up, because that would get them off their hands for a bit...It's normal: you're busy and you've got other priorities sometimes. You think, 'Oh, just get him locked up and

get him out of my hair!' We sometimes feel like that. We shouldn't do, but sometimes you just think, 'At least I've got a few weeks.' (YOT Worker)

It therefore stands to reason that professionals might not always project a particularly favourable impression of a young person to court. Alternatively, some of the professionals, who at times were required to accompany the young people to court, commented upon how they felt that they often could not provide an 'honest' account of the young person because they did not wish to alienate him or her:

> I've been to court on a few occasions, and I've had to stand up in Court, and tell the judge about the young person I'm with. And you're not going to turn round and tell the judge that he's a little brat or something like that and he needs locking up! You're going to gloss over it ... 'He's trying very hard!' That's happened a couple of times. (Residential Care Worker)

They expressed that because of this, the young people might potentially get away with things that an individual from a 'conventional' family might not. Whether this is in fact the case, is open to debate, given that parents might also be constrained from telling the 'truth' as they see it, due to the bonds of family loyalty, and/or a wish to minimise their own perceived deficits. In addition, the comments of some of the court professionals revealed that the workers were not always as successful in concealing their feelings as they might believe:

> What they have to say doesn't always go along with body language ... You can tell little things, you can tell. (Magistrate)
>
> I've seen the look on those care-workers faces; they feel very torn. They want to tell the court the truth about that child ... but they don't want to alienate that child, and they're in a very difficult position. (Legal Adviser)

Again, it is possible that such impressions could have a negative impact upon sentencing decisions. However, another magistrate commented how she felt that young people-care worker relationships were often of insufficient depth to merit the drawing of valid conclusions regarding the nature of the young people:

> Quite often, there's not that relationship there. I really feel that if they're on a bad day, or they've had to travel with them a long time, they're probably just fed up with them. And just because they're under so much pressure as well ... I wouldn't take as much into account as if it were their own parent. (Magistrate)

Indeed, the Magistrates Association Youth Courts Committee (2012, p.4) also expressed concern that Magistrates are seeing young people in court who are either unaccompanied or accompanied by a carer with minimal knowledge of the young person. This was again something that I experienced as a court officer and, rightly or wrongly, it served to create the impression of a lack of care and concern on the part of some children's homes: the young person seemingly abandoned to the youth justice system.

Conclusion

Overall, Foucault's (1977, p.301) assertion that, 'it is not on the fringes of society that criminality is born, but by means of ever more closely placed insertions, under ever more insistent surveillance, by an accumulation of disciplinary coercion ...' appears to have a certain resonance in the context of children's residential care. It is clear that the youth justice system is indeed seen by both children's home staff and 'front-line' social workers, as a useful and necessary adjunct to the care system: a legitimate and officially sanctioned 'coercive back-up' to enforce institutional authority (Donzelot, 1979). It is used to maintain the disciplinary power of residential children's homes, consequently criminalising already vulnerable children and young people.

The reasons for this are manifold and a number of interconnected themes predominate. These include widespread perceptions of the young people as being a difficult group in need of surveillance; control, punishment and moral guidance, at times via retributive means; the need to preserve the authority of the children's home and its staff and the lack of empowerment experienced by residential care staff, resulting in them being more likely to seek to manage challenging behaviour via the youth justice system.

When prosecuted, a young person's care status appears to have both positive and negative implications, with some discerning that they experience a greater leniency, and others feeling that they are penalised for perceived ingratitude towards those who are charged with their care. A lack of awareness and understanding regarding how the often negative pre- and in-care experiences of the young people impact upon their subsequent behaviour in the residential context was also at times in evidence and points to the need to raise awareness of such issues amongst those responsible for sentencing.

What is clear is that recourse to the youth justice system for minor incidents committed within the residential context is still all too common and serious thought needs to be given to how such reliance can be effectively challenged. In the concluding chapter, the connecting themes emerging from the research will be explored and potential directions for future policy discussed.

Part III
Conclusion

8
Key Findings and Implications for Policy and Practice

Introduction

This study confirms that there are a number of interconnecting influences which contribute to young people coming to the attention of the youth justice system while in residential care. This complex interplay of factors inevitably means that the task of reducing youth justice involvement will be far from straightforward. Nevertheless, the research provides a useful overview of how experiences both prior and subsequent to residence in a children's home could potentially shape the responses of residents; it also provides valuable insight regarding how the thought processes of professionals can contribute to the experiences of the young people and their consequent criminalisation. The study brings together both new and existing research findings and theories of human behaviour at the individual, institutional and wider systemic levels in order to facilitate insight into this particular issue. At the same time it has incorporated a consideration of relevant legislative, policy and practice initiatives. In this final chapter the key findings from the research are outlined, leaving little doubt that we still have some way to go in order to improve outcomes for the young people who get into trouble whilst in residential care. Recommendations for policy and practice are made, along with a brief discussion of future priorities in this area.

Key findings

At the individual level, pre-care experiences undoubtedly contribute to subsequent youth justice involvement: the young people's combined desire to overcome disempowerment experienced within their families and communities of origin and their need for 'social recognition' (Barry, 2006) often meant that the peer group came to replace immediate family, and adult influence, in terms of providing emotional support and a sense of self-worth and status. This at times resulted in youth justice involvement and was a factor which continued to be influential when the young people were later taken into care. Indeed, Emond's (2003) argument that the significance of their relationships with fellow residents should not be underestimated is clearly resonant and the question to consider is therefore how we can preserve and enhance the positive aspects of such relationships, while ensuring that the more negative elements (Polsky, 1962) are curtailed. The research suggests that careful thought should be given to the mix of residents in individual children's homes and how the dynamics of the resident group might potentially encourage or militate against troublesome behaviour.

Nevertheless, it is important that we do not allow a focus upon pre-care experiences and the relationships between individual young people to obscure other contributory factors. The differing cultures and characteristics of individual children's homes and associated interactions between staff and residents appear to be capable of producing both positive and negative outcomes; the young people experienced a variation in the quality of provision across both the public and private sectors. Good practice requires leadership in developing positive cultures in residential care (Whitaker, Archer and Hicks, 1998; Sinclair and Gibbs, 1998; Brown et al., 1998; Anglin, 2002) with 'clarity of roles and congruence in aims and objectives' (Kendrick, 2012, p.296). Rather than pursuing an authoritarian line which can produce resistance (Goffman, 1961; Foucault, 1978, 1977), staff should be approachable and willing to engage with the young people in a way that respects them as individuals, taking into account their personal histories, perspectives and life experiences (Clough, 2000). Discrete therapeutic approaches which encourage staff to engage meaningfully with the young people in this way seem to offer a positive way forward (Stevens and Furnivall, 2008) in a sector where the nature of care in many instances remains less than ideal.

Certainly, as argued by Clough, Bullock and Ward (2006, p.44) 'system neglect' whereby the needs of children remain unmet can be just as damaging as other forms of abuse, yet this is rarely acknowledged when the young people get into trouble. Irony can be found in the focus upon the perceived individual deficits of young people in both the care and youth justice systems, yet the needs of those individuals often seem to be marginalised by policy and practice. This is a state of affairs which runs counter to the spirit of both national and international legislation and edicts from the 1948 Children Act onwards, including the obligation placed upon local authorities to be good 'corporate parents'. Multiple placement moves resulting in the exacerbation or precipitation of both short and longer term psychological and emotional difficulties were all too common for some young people and the lack of heterogeneity in placements meant that units at times struggled to cope with the diverse needs that were presented: this particularly appeared to impact negatively upon outcomes for girls. Similarly, the placement of individuals in out of area, single-child or isolated units away from family and friends was often met with anger, frustration and ultimately resistance (Foucault, 1978), and while certain young people might benefit from such placements particularly in relation to safeguarding considerations, their use added to the impression of young people being moved 'out of sight, out of mind'.

Indeed, the study revealed how the perceptions of the professionals who work with the young people have the potential to profoundly impact upon their experiences whilst in residential care and subsequent outcomes. The 'individualization' of offending and troublesome behaviour by social workers and other professionals particularly when previous actions directed towards encouraging the young person to change appear to have failed often resulted in an unhelpfully punitive and retributive outlook colouring their responses. Such attitudes were further perpetuated by a lack of understanding of the young people, who had often developed non-mainstream childhood identities as a result of earlier experiences. This was in turn compounded by changes of social worker and an invariably distant working relationship inherent in both the case-management approach to intervention and the geographical spread of placements. Similarly, the propensity of some staff to rely upon police intervention within the residential context reveals a perception of the young people as being primarily a difficult group in need of surveillance and control (Foucault, 1977; Donzelot, 1979) combined with a real lack of empowerment and confidence in their own abilities to successfully deal with presenting issues.

What is clear is that rather than simply focusing upon the discourses of individual culpability and responsibility when the young people get into trouble, it is necessary to employ an holistic approach which both recognises and focuses on the contribution of values and identities formed by the young people prior to entering residential care, the importance of peer relationships, the impact of staff-resident relationships as well as the institutional culture and environment, overarching policy and practice and the perceptions of professionals. Only in this way can we hope to make realistic progress in addressing youth justice involvement in a way which will be of benefit to the greatest number of children and young people.

Recent developments

At the time of writing, government interest in improving outcomes in the care system appears to be particularly strong, following on from the previous administration's efforts via the Care Matters process (DfES, 2006; DfES, 2007). As recently as June 2013, children's minister Edward Timpson announced a package of reforms of children's residential care with the aim of tackling what were termed 'system-wide failings'. It was stated that under the proposed changes, Ofsted (the Office for Standards in Education, Children's Services and Skills) will refuse to let new homes open in areas deemed to be unsafe and existing homes in unsafe areas will face closure if they cannot demonstrate that they can protect children. Certainly, in light of recent criminal cases involving the abuse and exploitation of vulnerable girls, such as those in Rochdale, these measures seem to be particularly appropriate. However, the question of what criteria will be utilised in order to determine whether an area is 'safe' or otherwise and exactly how effective that will be remains to be seen. In addition, care home workers will be required to meet a minimum level qualification within a set period of time and, 'to improve transparency', full inspection reports of homes will be published along with details of who owns the home unless that risks identifying children.

Importantly, from January 2014, there is to be a requirement that Directors of Children's Services must ensure 'robust processes' are in place for the challenge and scrutiny of decisions to place a child 'out of area' (Puffett, 2014). While a high quality 'out of area' placement can be both beneficial for and welcomed by some young people, it was certainly the case that during the course of this study, the potentially damaging effects of moving a young person away from friends and family were demonstrated, particularly when the young person felt that their wishes in respect of this were being ignored.

Of course as with so many previous initiatives, the devil will again be in the detail and, as evidenced amply by the research findings, what constitutes a child's best interests may well be a point of contention between young people and the adults who are responsible for their care. It will also unquestionably be the case that what will be deemed to constitute 'robust processes' will link directly to the policy's effectiveness, as will the availability of resources to meet children's needs closer to home in the current climate of financial austerity. Indeed, the Children and Young Persons Act 2008 included a new general duty on local authorities to place a child with a relative, near their home, and with siblings (if they are also in care) as well as taking steps to ensure the availability of sufficient accommodation that is appropriate for the needs of the children and young people they look after within their local authority area (unless that is inconsistent with a child's welfare). Nonetheless, as demonstrated by the latest proposals, the issues which these provisions were intended to tackle remain as problematic as ever. Indeed, while successive administrations have indicated their intentions to improve the residential care sector, it would appear that the battle to overcome its residual status is far from over, as evidenced by the current government's recent announcement that from April 2014, young people will be able to stay with their foster carers until they are 21 if they and their carers agree. However (unlike in Scotland), a similar level of support will not currently be offered to young people in residential care, who all too often have to leave before they are ready (The Who Cares Trust, 2013).

Certainly, while it has been shown that being in care can benefit many (see Berridge et al., 2008; Forrester et al., 2007), it is clear from the findings of this study that far more significant and wide-reaching reforms will be required in order to effectively improve experiences and outcomes (including a reduction in youth justice system contact) for a significant minority of individuals in residential care. Therefore, on the basis of the findings, there are various recommendations to be made that are relevant to policy and practice. Although the Coalition government has expressed a welcome commitment to improving the residential care sector and the experiences of the children and young people within it, there is much work still to do.

Recommendations for policy and practice

Promote social justice

Social justice can be defined as the fair distribution of wealth, opportunities and privileges within a society and is something which successive UK governments have claimed to promote. Nevertheless, inequality and poverty remain ever present, with research persuasively demonstrating that such factors generate poor outcomes across a range of social indicators (i.e. Wilkinson and Pickett, 2009) and can have both a direct and indirect impact upon a child's reception into care and subsequent behaviour. Certainly, as highlighted by Francis (2008, p.221), the families of children who come into care are characterised by poverty and unemployment, marital discord and breakdown, inadequate housing and over-crowding, health problems and social isolation. This was undoubtedly the case for the majority of the young people who participated in this study and it was such factors that had directly and indirectly contributed to their initial involvement with the youth justice system.

Furthermore, the 2013 Care Inquiry highlighted how the context of people's lives is worsening, precipitated by the economic slowdown, financial austerity and concomitant increases in poverty; unemployment and changes to the benefit system which have put additional strain on families in difficulties. These developments do not bode well for those individuals who are growing up in such circumstances and as children in care are, almost exclusively, children of the poor and marginalised, underpinning all discussions about them should be a focus on the impact of inequality. Certainly, while successive UK governments may aspire to secure social justice and to tackle child poverty in particular, there is clearly still a long way to go. Both current and previous strategies have preserved the current economic model and neglected to address the all-pervasive systemic inequalities that exist within society and effect the structural change which it can be argued is essential to deliver true social justice (Silver, 2012). It is therefore the duty of society and those who are responsible for social policy, to consider how social justice can be promoted via redistributive strategies, and positive, practical steps taken to ensure that families are not placed under further pressure in these times of economic hardship.

Indeed, it can be argued that the care system is in many ways a measure of social policy and attitudes towards children and their families. Where they are undervalued, stigmatised and marginalised this is reflected in the nature of the care system – as we saw with the Rumanian orphanages under Communism. However, where such children and families are valued and invested in we tend to find more caring and successful care systems – as in many Northern European countries (Shaw and Frost, 2013). A move towards a 'robust system of social justice' (ibid., p.146) is therefore both desirable and advantageous for all children and young people.

Invest in family support

Alongside a strong and successful system of social justice, there is still the need to help those in difficulty and indeed, many of the young people who participated in this research were admitted into care in times of crisis following the breakdown of family relationships. The Munro Review of Child Protection (2011, p.7) 'noted the growing body of evidence of the effectiveness of early intervention' with such families, stating that 'preventive services can do more to reduce abuse and neglect than reactive services'. This contention has been recently endorsed by the Association of Directors of Children's Services Ltd (ADCS, 2013) and clearly highlights a need for further investment in family support services, rather than the worrying reduction in funding that has been precipitated by recent public spending cuts. Certainly, in terms of children 'on the edge of care', a concept which refers to those children and young people who are identified as being in real and imminent risk of entering the care system (Shaw and Frost, 2013), Ofsted undertook a study which was very positive about the potential impact of services:

> Without exception, all the young people and parents spoken to were very clear about the difference the support had made to their

lives. For some the impact had been significant and they felt that their lives had been turned around. (Ofsted, 2011, p.12)

Many of the young people were judged to have been living in 'poor home conditions, often for long periods of time' (ibid., p.13). The outcomes, in terms of avoiding care, were successful in all of the studied cases, with the report concluding that 'it was the quality of the professional involved, significantly the key professional, which was the crucial factor in helping to achieve success' (ibid., p. 4; Shaw and Frost, 2013). The services had the following features:

- Strong multi-agency working both operationally and strategically,
- Clear and consistent referral pathways,
- Clearly understood and consistent decision-making processes based on thorough assessment of risks and strengths of the family network,
- A prompt, persistent, and flexible approach, which was based on listening to the views of the young person and the family and building on their strengths,
- A clear plan of work based on thorough assessment and mutually agreed goals: regular review of progress and risk factors; robust and understood arrangements between agencies in respect of risk management; and clear planning for case closure and for sustainability of good outcomes (Ofsted, 2011, p.5).

Potentially, therefore, a clearly conceptualised and well-resourced and targeted family support system can help in working with children and young people on the edge of care and in helping to reduce the need for admission to the system, something which would have been of great benefit to a number of the young people in this study.

Nonetheless, the form that preventive intervention should take has been a source of contention with one of the government's latest high profile initiatives – the 'Troubled Families' programme – attracting criticism for its definition of a 'troubled family'; the reliability of the figures used as a basis for the programme (Levitas, 2012) and the fact that the government expects councils to fund their contributions from existing budgets at a time when council budgets are being slashed and funding to family intervention projects were being reduced.

Undoubtedly, the coverage of previous similar initiatives have been by no means comprehensive despite substantial financial investment and it will remain to be seen whether the scheme reaps dividends in terms of improving the lives of children and young people who might otherwise be at risk of being taken into care.

Keep placement changes to a minimum

Schofield et al. (2012) found that a system is effective at promoting good care when it promotes security, resilience and pro-social relationships. Whether the reason for moving a child is financially or behaviourally led, planned or otherwise, the findings of this study strongly support the contention that multiple placement changes can be extremely damaging for already vulnerable individuals (see also Munro and Hardy, 2007) often resulting in the perpetuation and precipitation of challenging behaviour. As a consequence of this, steps should be taken to ensure that such moves only occur when absolutely necessary, a proposition that will require both a genuine commitment to prioritising child welfare over financial imperatives and rethinking the risk averse approach to 'troublesome' young people in care which often predominates, whereby problems are 'managed rather than necessarily resolved' (Muncie, 2000, p.29).

Such ingrained outlooks will be far from easy to overcome, particularly at a time when local authority budgets are being cut and social services departments (and children's homes), judged upon their ability to promote successful outcomes, are in ever present danger of being penalised when things go wrong. However, it is clearly the duty of a corporate parent to ensure as stable an upbringing as possible for those in its care and indeed in relation to those individuals who display challenging behaviour, the value of homes 'not giving up' is certainly endorsed by this study. This can produce benefits in terms of behavioural improvement and ultimately in supporting the formation of secure, positive relationships so vital to their short- and longer-term well-being (Schofield et al., 2012) and arguably, their propensity to lead a law-abiding life. As such, an inspection regime which assesses 'progress' relative to the needs of each individual child, would undoubtedly be advantageous. Of course, placement breakdowns can also occur when a young person has been poorly matched to a particular home and as discussed in the following section, a primary reason for this lies in the lack of availability and homogeneity of residential provision so prevalent across the public, private and voluntary sectors.

Increase the availability and heterogeneity of residential provision

Previous research reveals that children's homes are the preferred option of many young people (Sinclair and Gibbs, 1998; Anglin and Knorth, 2004) and recent government pronouncements have indicated that residential care should be seen by local authorities as a positive placement option rather than a last resort (House of Commons, 2011). However, this study supports the contention that the lack of diversity in residential provision means that young people (often adolescent entrants to the care system) are sometimes placed in homes which are ill-equipped to meet their needs, consequently resulting in further troublesome behaviour and recourse to the youth justice system. Indeed, the Association of Directors of Children's Services Ltd (ADCS, 2013, p.3) highlights how research indicates that, 'we need a range of care provision to address the heterogeneity of the adolescent care population, addressing age...placement history and reasons for entering care'. The current research indicates that to this it might also be pertinent to add the need to address a young person's differential requirements as dictated by gender (see also O'Neill, 2008).

Current homogeneity is as a direct consequence of the lack of investment in the residential care sector over a number of years, leaving a largely generic private sector service which is often located in areas where housing is inexpensive (creating an uneven geographical spread of resources) and tries to have as broad an appeal as possible, thus maximising its profitability. The more specialised provision which does exist is invariably extremely expensive and limited. Thus, an overall expansion of the sector, with public, private and voluntary providers being financially incentivised to increase their range of provision would seem to be the way forward. This would pave the way not only for the needs of young people to be catered for more successfully, but would also mean fewer young people having to be placed at great distances form their family and friends, other than for safeguarding reasons.

Improve overall quality of residential care

The research findings reaffirmed the acknowledged variability of the quality of care provided by residential children's homes with both positive and negative experiences reported across the public and private sectors. Ofsted inspections of children's homes similarly paint a varied picture of the sector and indeed, of the 1,986 children's homes run by local authorities and independent sector providers to have undergone full inspections between April 2012 and March 2013, only 309 (16 per cent) were classed as outstanding, with 56 per cent assessed as being 'good', 24 per cent classed as 'satisfactory/adequate' and 5 per cent (103) assessed as inadequate (Hayes, 2013). This is certainly far from ideal and provides further evidence that there is a long way to go in terms of producing consistently high standards.

Although there is no single model of provision which could meet the needs of such a diverse population of children and young people, as explored at various points in this book, research has revealed certain fundamental factors which have been found to contribute to improved outcomes (Kendrick, 2012, p. 296; Whitaker, Archer and Hicks, 1998; Sinclair and Gibbs, 1998; Berridge and Brodie, 1998; Brown et al., 1998; Hicks et al., 2007; Anglin, 2002) including 'child centred' practice, and indeed the Munro Review of Child Protection (2011) recommended that as well as focusing upon processes, inspections should also look at outcomes and how children's wishes and experiences shape services provided.

In June 2013, Ofsted revealed that – following a consultation – 'adequate' ratings are to be replaced with a new 'requires improvement' rating. In addition it launched three consultations (14.6.13) on the way it inspects children's social care services – all three of which describe 'good' as the minimum standard children, families and carers should expect. The first consultation set out Ofsted's plans for a single framework for child protection inspections and the inspecting of services for care leavers and children in care, due to take effect in November 2013. If a council is judged to be inadequate in any of Ofsted's three key inspection areas – the experiences and progress of children who need help and protection; the experiences and progress of children in care and achieving permanence for them; leadership, management and governance – it will automatically be rated 'inadequate' for overall effectiveness (Ofsted, 2013; Pemberton, 2013).

However, it is arguable that without increased investment in the residential sector and raising awareness amongst practitioners and providers regarding what constitutes effective practice, local authorities will struggle to bring overall standards up to a consistently acceptable level. Indeed, as things currently stand, financially struggling councils often choose to either close children's homes or 'drive a hard bargain on the price of placements' (Cooper, 2013), thus mitigating against the provision of quality care. Therefore, along with a much needed financial boost, the work of the Children's Homes Challenge and Improvement Programme could be built upon and extended and indeed, Jonathan Stanley, Chief Executive of the Independent Children's Home Association (ICHA) has been critical of Ofsted for not taking on more of an development role that might help failing homes improve more rapidly, stating that it makes sense for them to distribute data on where good practice is and what it is achieving (Cooper, 2013).

Furthermore, concerns have been raised by Mark Rogers, the Society of Local Authority Chief Executives' (SOLACE) lead on children's services, about the capability of Ofsted to produce a rigorous, consistent standard of inspection which is grounded in the experience of children and their families, stating that inspections are still relying too heavily upon a box-ticking, process driven approach, 'which punishes innovation at the expense of high quality care' (Wiggins, 2013). Certainly, the Care Inquiry (2013) highlights how focusing on quality requires greater clarity about the desired outcomes for a particular child and about ways of measuring progress towards achieving those outcomes, including measuring less tangible outcomes concerning children's well-being (ibid., p.7). Subsequently, amendments were introduced to the Children and Families Bill 2013 being considered at the time of writing by the House of Lords that will enable the development of a revised inspection framework for children's homes based on quality standards that all homes must aspire to:

These changes aim to facilitate a move away from a regulation and inspection framework that rests on national minimum standards to one that sets high standards for children in residential care and offers them support to achieve positive outcomes. (The Children's Partnership, 2013, p.1)

It has been highlighted that the Department for Education aims to work with key partners in 2014 to develop these standards which it is hoped will strip away much of the 'current overly bureaucratic framework', facilitate increased discretion and encourage innovation in the sector (ibid., p.1). It will remain to be seen whether the proposed changes will produce tangible improvements. Nevertheless, the desirability of focusing upon the needs of individual children and young people is something which is further emphasised in the following recommendation.

Encourage 'child-centred' practice

The findings of this research consistently highlighted the need to work with young people in ways which situate them and their experiences at the centre of practice. Indeed, from decisions regarding the most appropriate placement for a young person, through to everyday interactions with them in the residential context, to how professional's respond when they get into trouble, the need to take into account the young person's history and perspectives is vital to building positive relationships; achieving cooperation and ultimately, securing successful outcomes. Furthermore, this suggests that rather than reacting with frustration, negativity and punitive responses when young people fail to cooperate with interventions or continue to get into trouble, a more productive way forward lies in considering the reasons behind their actions and taking into account what they feel would be the best way forward. Indeed, McLeod (2007) argues that:

A prerequisite for adults working with disaffected youth is sensitivity towards issues of power and an understanding of how powerlessness can shape the responses of those who are marginalized. Those who wish to listen to young people must be prepared for resistance and challenge, they must be flexible enough to be open to the unexpected, and confident enough to allow their own assumptions to be questioned. (McLeod, 2007, p.285)

Establishing a more 'child-centred' outlook may be difficult to achieve in a bureaucratic, financially restricted, risk-averse environment and indeed, the Munro Review of Child Protection lamented the existence of a 'defensive system that puts so much emphasis on procedures and recording that insufficient attention is given to developing and supporting the expertise to work effectively with children, young people and families' (Munro, 2011, p.6). Nevertheless, as will be explored further in the next recommendation, the findings of this study support the contention that encouraging and facilitating such practice amongst professionals involved in working with young people in residential care is undoubtedly the way forward.

On a related note, McNeill et al. (2005) identified three approaches to work with offenders which they implied could be relevant in promoting behavioural change and reducing problematic behaviour across the board in the social work, as well as the criminal/youth justice arena. These were:

- Accurate empathy, respect or warmth and therapeutic genuineness;
- Establishing a therapeutic relationship involving mutual understanding and agreement about the nature and purpose of intervention;
- Person centred and collaborative working, taking into account the client's perspective and using the client's concepts.

Such approaches could be utilised both by social workers in the context of case work (rather than case-management) relationships, and (as advocated by the discrete therapeutic approaches previously discussed) residential care staff in individual children's homes in order to promote improved outcomes. However, as touched upon earlier, effective implementation will require a rethink of the way that front-line social services are currently administered, with greater importance placed upon the child-worker relationship. The need to reduce placement moves in order to promote the formation of secure, positive relationships has already been discussed and in addition to this, it would be pertinent to stress the potential importance of a strong, consistent and supportive social worker presence in the lives of young people. Indeed, the Care Inquiry (2013) recently recommended that local authorities should try to achieve a good match between child and social worker and give serious consideration to the child's request for a change in social worker. Conversely, where relationships are good, a real effort should be made to ensure that social workers are not changed unless absolutely necessary and the Inquiry recommended that the maintenance of contact should be encouraged if the worker changes jobs; the child changes placement or leaves care. Furthermore, as professionals who feel disempowered are less likely to listen to and respect young people (Smith, 2009a), the re-empowerment, re-education and re-training of many professionals is clearly necessary.

Encourage and facilitate professional empowerment and expertise

Following on from the themes explored in the prior recommendation, it was noticeable how a sense of powerlessness in terms of dealing with troublesome behaviour and presenting issues pervaded the responses of many of the professionals in this study. As previously stated, this manifested in the frustration of social workers who then went on to advocate punitive, controlling responses to persistent misbehaviour, and residential care staff who relied heavily upon a police presence and youth justice intervention. The Munro Review of Child Protection Final Report (2011, pp.7–8) argues that the level of increased prescription for social workers, while intended to improve the quality of practice, has created an imbalance; compliance with prescription and keeping records to demonstrate compliance has become too dominant:

> The centrality of forming relationships with children and families to understand and help them has become obscured...Building on the work of the Social Work Task Force (SWTF) and the Social Work Reform Board (SWRB), this review makes the case for radically improving the knowledge and skills of social workers from initial training through to continuing professional development. (ibid., p.8)

Thus, a system which nurtures and values professional expertise is advocated; a reduction in central prescription to help professionals move away from a compliance culture to a learning culture, 'where they have more freedom to use their expertise in assessing need and providing the right help' (ibid., p.7). While increasing workforce expertise will require investment, it is highlighted how in areas where local reforms have upgraded the knowledge and skills of their workforce, savings have been seen overall (ibid., p.8).

Similarly, the study clearly highlighted the sense of disempowerment felt by many front-line children's home staff. Although Sinclair and Gibbs (1998) could find no evidence that a better-qualified staff group in itself predicted better outcomes, high quality training and opportunities for continuing professional development, are clearly two of many important factors essential to achieving successful practice when working with children who are often both vulnerable and present challenging behaviour. Clough, Bullock and Ward (2006) highlight how professional qualifying training has not been widely available to residential workers since the demise of the certificate of social service (CSS) programmes nearly 30 years ago. They argue that while vocational qualifications (the level 3 Diploma in Children and Young People's Workforce is currently the qualification that someone starting in the workforce today would be expected to gain) offer a reasonable introduction to the basics of the work, they should not be confused with a recognised *professional qualification* and need to be accompanied by a 'much more sophisticated programme of staff training and development' (ibid., p.50). The recognised professional qualification for working in residential child care has been a diploma in social work (DipSW), or one of its predecessors, with the UK being the only European country which sees social work as the core professional discipline for this sector, a state of affairs which has progressively attracted criticism:

> Increasingly many in the UK have argued that...social work training does not adequately prepare people for working in residential establishments and is not the proper professional base for residential practice...First, too often it fails to equip staff for the work they have to do. Second, residential social workers with a generic field and residential qualification are more likely to move out of residential work than are field workers to move in. (Clough, Bullock and Ward, 2006, p.50)

Consequently, only a very small proportion of qualifying social workers opt to work in residential care, something which is no doubt also linked to the relatively poor status of the sector (see below). Residential staff have continued to perceive social work courses as insufficiently geared to their training needs, with '(for example) very little focus on group living and group work, or on ways of handling issues arising in daily living' (ibid.). The Report of the Expert Group on the Quality of children's homes, presented to Department for Education Ministers in December 2012 and published in April 2013 (DfE, 2013d), highlighted both how it has been suggested that a vocational qualification specific to children's residential care would be more appropriate and that there has been a growing interest in foundation degrees being a way of raising the skills and qualification level of the workforce. However, few relevant courses are currently available at either undergraduate or postgraduate level, with an exception being the Master's level qualification in Advanced Residential Childcare offered at the University of Strathclyde in association with the Centre for Excellence for Looked After Children in Scotland (CELCIS). Tellingly, the website states that the course is unique in the British Isles in offering a Masters level award specifically in residential care.

Along with stating that care home workers will be required to meet a minimum level qualification within a set period of time, children's minister Edward Timpson in May 2013 announced a comprehensive review of the training, qualifications and career pathways for new and existing staff in children's homes, which will inform the development of a training and qualifications framework. It is to be hoped that these developments will result in much needed improvements to the confidence and ability of the workforce to deal with presenting issues.

Indeed, unlike other western European nations, that educate their social pedagogues to graduate level, residential care work in the UK is not accorded a particularly high status and, 'heavy workloads, poor pay...and poor supervision impact on turnover rates on both sides of the Atlantic' (Colton and Roberts, 2007). In addition, they are accorded little professional autonomy and rely heavily upon 'expert' intervention. It stands to reason that inadequate support and training, resulting in a lack of confidence and a consequent inability to handle difficult situations in the context of a risk-averse, highly bureaucratic system (Berridge et al., 2011) will result in an increased propensity to resort to the youth justice system. It has been found that the workforce generally feel undervalued and not well understood by wider society, linked to poor public understanding and perceptions of children's homes as a whole. As well as having a negative impact on recruitment and retention, this also makes it difficult for staff in homes to be strong advocates on behalf of children in multi-agency conversations (DfE, 2013d). These are clearly issues which need to be addressed across the private, public and voluntary sectors in order to effect change. They require a commitment to building and maintaining a high quality, well trained, appropriately remunerated workforce that is supported and empowered to develop effective relationships with young people and deal with presenting issues. In addition, the need to improve public understanding of residential care as a whole, particularly in terms of the role and impact of its workforce and residential care as a career (DfE, 2013d) is of great importance.

Reconsider youth justice policy and practice

While the current research explored a period before the abolition of the OBTJ Target (see Chapter 2) and the restoration of increased discretion to front-line police ranks in the wake of the Legal Aid Sentencing and Punishment of Offenders Act 2012 will have had chance to take effect, it is clearly the case that young people in children's homes will, for the reasons explored, continue to have a greater propensity to come to the attention of the youth justice system than other children and young people. The questions of what should constitute an offence worthy of involving the police and what in turn should merit grounds for the prosecution of a residential-home based offence were discussed in the previous chapter and merit serious further consideration. However, Taylor (2006, p.184) goes further by arguing that,

> Youth justice policies should be urgently reviewed and joined up with welfare-based policies relating to young people in care. This is particularly important for youth justice measures that treat children in trouble primarily as offenders rather than as children in need.

Here Taylor commends the Scottish system: an approach to youth justice which, while not perfect and has been the subject of some criticism (see McAra and McVie, 2010, pp.198–199), prioritises the welfare of children in trouble and has endured for over 30 years with no apparent rise in the crime rate (Smith, 2000). However, given the damaging impact that system contact has been found to have on young people (e.g. Tracy and Kempf-Leonard, 1996; Huizinga et al., 2003; McAra and McVie, 2007), it is arguable that policy development should go even further by raising the age of criminal responsibility to at least the mid-teens in line with the many other European countries. While this would not exclude all young people in residential care, it would mean that a significant number would be prevented from entering the youth justice system at a younger age, thus decreasing the likelihood of amplifying rather than diminishing offending in the longer-term (e.g. Tracy and Kempf-Leonard, 1996; Huizinga et al., 2003; McAra and McVie, 2007).

Conclusion

In light of the research presented in this book, a key question that would certainly be worthy of further investigation is how girls specifically respond to the residential care environment; how they are responded to by staff; how their needs may be different from those of boys; and whether alternative approaches and policies are required in order to maximise their chances of achieving a positive outcome. It would also be illuminating to explore the accounts of those who did not offend whilst in residential care and experienced positive outcomes. Comparing and contrasting their voices with those who did get into trouble in order to discern what lessons might usefully be learned would undoubtedly add greater depth to existing knowledge. Furthermore, there is clearly a need to raise awareness amongst those involved in youth sentencing of the issues facing children and young people in residential care in order to allay misconceptions and promote the most appropriate responses.

This study has drawn upon the voices of young people who have offended whilst in residential care and the professionals who work with them in the care and youth justice systems in order to illuminate the reasons why individuals in residential care might get into trouble. It has been argued that along with their pre-care circumstances, factors directly linked to their care experiences have the potential to exacerbate existing problems or create new ones, with the needs of individual young people often lost. This means that in certain respects, local authorities have failed to successfully discharge their duty as corporate parents in accordance with the spirit of various legislative and policy initiatives. At the time of writing, the government has stated its intention to improve outcomes in the residential care sector and acknowledged that rigidly drawing young people into the youth justice system is not always appropriate or necessary. However, without substantial investment throughout the sector, including in the establishment of a confident and empowered workforce, and replacing the bureaucratic, risk-averse mentality that currently dominates practice with a 'child-centred' ethos, local authorities will continue to struggle to discharge their responsibilities and young people will suffer the effects of this. Research, including the current study, has revealed some encouraging examples of residential care practice both nationally and internationally and reported positive accounts of the benefits of such provision from young people (Emond, 2003; Berridge et al., 2008; Morgan, 2009). It is our duty as a society to ensure that a much needed resource is given the support it requires to be consistently excellent in order that it can benefit our most vulnerable and troubled children and young people, thus reducing the likelihood of youth justice contact.

References

ADCS (2013) *The Association of Directors of Children's Services Ltd Position Statement: What is Care For: Alternative Models of Care for Adolescents* (April 2013), www.adcs.org.uk/download/position-statements/2013/ADCS_position_statement_What_Is_Care_For_April_2013.pdf (URL last accessed on 27.8.13).

Allen, R. (2011) *Last Resort? Exploring the Reduction in Child Imprisonment 2008–11*, Prison Reform Trust, www.prisonreformtrust.org.uk/Portals/0/Documents/lastresort.pdf (URL last accessed on 27.4.13).

Anglin, J.P. (2002) *Pain, Normality and the Struggle for Congruence: Reinterpreting Residential Care for Children and Youth*, Binghamton, NY: The Haworth Press.

Anglin, J. and Knorth, E. (2004) Competing declarations on residential care for children and youth–Stockholm versus Malmo: international perspectives on rethinking residential care, *Child and Youth Care Forum*, 33(3), 141–149.

APPG (2012) The All Party Parliamentary Group for Runaway and Missing Children and Adults and the All Party Parliamentary Group for Looked After Children and Care Leavers–Report from the Joint Inquiry into Children who go Missing from Care, June 2012, https://www.gov.uk/government/uploads/system/uploads/attachment-data/file/1775563/Report_-_children_who_go_missing_from_care_pdf (URL last accessed on 27.8.13).

Barry, M. (2006) *Youth Offending in Transition: The Search for Social Recognition*, Oxon: Routledge.

Barter, C. (2008) Prioritising Young People's Concerns in Residential Care: Responding to Peer Violence. In Kendrick, A. (ed.) *Residential Child Care: Prospects and Challenges*, London: Jessica Kingsley, pp.137–151.

Barter, C., Renold, E., Berridge, D. and Cawson, P. (2004) *Peer Violence in Children's Residential Care*, Hampshire: Palgrave.

Bateman, T. (2011) Child imprisonment: exploring 'injustice by geography'. Prison Service Journal, September 2011, No 197, Special Edition: Young People in Custody.

Bell, M. (2002) Promoting children's rights through the use of relationship. *Child and Family Social Work*, 7, 1–11. Quoted in McLeod, A. (2007) Whose agenda? Issues of power and relationship when listening to looked after young people, *Child and Family Social Work*, 12(3), 278–286.

Berridge, D. (2002) Residential Care. In McNeish, D., Newman, T. and Roberts, H. (eds) *What Works for Children?* Buckingham: Open University Press, pp.83–104.

Berridge, D. and Brodie, I. (1998) *Children's Homes Revisited*, London: Jessica Kingsley Publishers.

Berridge, D., Biehal, N. and Henry, L. (2012) *Living in Children's Residential Homes* (Research Report), London: Department for Education.

Berridge, D., Biehal, N., Lutman, E., Henry, L. and Palomares, M. (2011) *Raising the Bar? Evaluation of the Social Pedagogy Pilot Programme*, London: Department for Education.

Berridge, D., Dance, C., Beecham, J. and Field, S. (2008) *Educating Difficult Adolescents. Effective Education for Children in Public Care or with Emotional and Behavioural Difficulties*, London: Jessica Kingsley Publishers.

Biehal, N. (2005) *Working with Adolescents: Supporting Families, Preventing Breakdown*, London: BAAF.

Biehal, N. and Wade, J. (2000) Going missing from residential and foster care: linking biographies and contexts, *British Journal of Social Work*, 30, 211–225.

Biehal, N., Clayden, M., Stein, M. and Wade, J. (1995) *Moving On: Young People and Leaving Care Schemes*, London: HMSO.

Blair, T. (1999) *Beveridge Revisited: A Welfare State for the 21st Century*. Lecture by the Prime Minister delivered at Toynbee Hall, 18th March.

Blumer, H. (1954) What is wrong with social theory? *American Sociological Review*, 19(1), 3–10. Quoted in Bryman, A. (1998) *Quantity and Quality in Social Research*, London: Routledge.

Bowlby, J. (1953) *Child Care and the Growth of Love*, Baltimore: Pelican.

British Society of Criminology (2006) *Code of Ethics for Researchers in the Field of Criminology*, London: BSC.

Brodie, I. (2001) *Children's Homes and Social Exclusion: Redefining the problem*, London: Jessica Kingsley Publishers.

Brodie, I. and Morris, M. (2009) *Improving Educational Outcomes for Looked-after Children and Young People*, London: C4EO.

Bromley, D. (1993) *Reputation, Image and Impression Management*, Chichester: Wiley. Quoted in Barry, M. (2006) *Youth Offending in Transition: The Search for Social Recognition*. Oxon: Routledge.

Brown, E., Bullock, R., Hobson, C. and Little, M. (1998) *Making Residential Care Work: Structure and Culture in Children's Homes*, Aldershot: Ashgate.

Bryman, A. (1988) *Quantity and Quality in Social Research*, London: Routledge.

Cameron, C., Bennert, K., Simon, A. and Wigfall, V. (2007) *Using Health, Education, Housing and Other Services: A Study of Care Leavers and Young People in Difficulty*, London: Thomas Coram Research Unit.

Care Inquiry (2013) *Making Not Breaking: Building Relationships for our Most Vulnerable Children: Findings and Recommendations of the Care Inquiry.* Launched in the House of Commons on 30 April 2013, www.fostering.net/sites/www.fostering.net/files/resources/reports/care-inquiry-full-report-april-2013.pdf (URL last accessed 8.8.13).

Carter, I. (2007) *It's Never Too Early…It's Never Too Late – The ACPO Strategy for Children and Young People*, London: ACPO.

Cassen, R. and Kingdon, G. (2007) *Tackling Low Educational Achievement*, York: Joseph Rowntree Foundation.

Cliffe, D. and Berridge, D. (1991) *Closing Children's Homes: An End to Residential Child Care?* London: National Children's Bureau.

Clough, R. (2000) *The Practice of Residential Work*, Basingstoke: Macmillan.

Clough, R., Bullock, R. and Ward, A. (2006) *What Works in Residential Child Care: A Review of the Research Evidence and the Practical Considerations*, London: National Children's Bureau.

Colton, M. (1988) Substitute care practice, *Adoption and Fostering*, 12, 30–34.

Colton, M. and Roberts, S. (2007) Factors that contribute to high turnover among residential child care staff, *Child and Family Social Work*, 12(2), 133–142.

Cooper, J. (2013) *How are Children's Homes Responding to Criticism and an Uncertain Future?* Community Care, 4.7.13, http://www.communitycare. co.uk/articles/04/07/2013.119305/how-are-childrens-homes-responding-to-criticism-and-an-uncertain-future.htm (URL last accessed 4.8.13).

Courtney, M.E., Tolev, T. and Gilligan, R. (2009) Looking backwards to see forwards clearly: a cross-national perspective on residential care. In Courtney, M.E. and Iwaniec, D. (eds) *Residential Care of Children: Comparative Perspectives*, Oxford: Oxford University Press.

CPS Legal Guidance (undated) www.cps.gov.uk/legal/v_to _z/youth _offenders/.

Darker, I., Ward, H. and Caulfield, L. (2008) An analysis of offending by young people looked after by local authorities, *Youth Justice*, 8(2), 134–148.

Denscombe, M. (2003) *The Good Research Guide*, Maidenhead: Open University Press.

Department for Communities and Local Government (DCLG) (2013) *Helping Troubled Families Turn their Lives Around*, http://www.gov.uk/governemnt/poli-cies/helping-troubled-families-turn-their-lives-around, updated 12 February 2013 (URL last accessed on 5.8.13).

Department for Communities and Local Government (DCLG) (2012) *The Troubled Families programme – Financial Framework for the Troubled Families Programme's Payment – by – Results Scheme for Local Authorities*, http www. gov.uk/government/publications/the-troubled-families-programme-finan-cial-framework (URL last accessed on 29.12.13).

Department for Education (DfE) (2013a) *Children's Homes Data Pack: 13 September 2013*, www.education.gov.uk.

Department for Education (DfE) (2013b) *Children Act 1989 Guidance and Regulations Volume 5: Children's Homes*, Updated 19 March 2013, www. education.gov.uk/aboutdfe/statutory/g00222870/children-act-1989-child-rens-homes (URL last accessed on 27.8.13).

Department for Education (DfE) (2013c) *Statistical First Release: Children looked after in England (including adoption and care leavers) Year Ending 31 March 2013*, London: Department for Education, https://www.gov.uk/govern-ment/organisations/department-for-education/series/statistics-looked-af-ter-children (URL last accessed 21.12.13).

Department for Education (DfE) (2013d) *Report of the Expert Group on the Quality of Children's Homes*, presented to DfE Ministers–December 2012, www.nationalarchives.gov.uk.

Department for Education (DfE) (2013e) *Outcomes for Children Looked After by Local Authorities in England: 31 March 2013*, https://www.gov.uk/govern-ment/organisations/department-for-education/series/statistics-looked-af-ter-children (URL last accessed on 4.1.14).

Department for Education (DfE) (2012a) *Children's Homes in England Data Pack: The Children: Data as at 31 March 2011*, March 2012, www.education. gov.uk.

Department for Education (DfE) (2012b) *Children's Homes Regulations, Guidance and National Minimum Standards*, updated 26.4.12, www.education.gov. uk/childrenandyoungpeople/families/childrenincare/childrenshomes/ a00191997/childrens-homes-regulations-guidance-and-national-minimum-standards (URL last accessed on 27.8.13).

Department for Education and Skills (2003) *Every Child Matters: The Green Paper*, Norwich: The Stationary Office.

Department for Education and Skills (2004) *Every Child Matters: The Next Steps*, Norwich: The Stationary Office.

Department for Education and Skills (DfES) (2006) *Care Matters: Transforming the Lives of Children and Young People in Care*, Norwich: The Stationary Office.

Department for Education and Skills (DfES) (2007) *Care Matters: Time for Change*, Norwich: The Stationary Office.

Department for Work and Pensions (DWP) (2012) *Social Justice: Transforming Lives*, Norwich: The Stationary Office.

Department for Work and Pensions and Department for Education (DWP and DfE) (2011) *A New Approach to Child Poverty: Tackling the Causes of Disadvantage and Transforming Families' Lives*, Norwich: The Stationary Office.

Donzelot, J. (1979) *The Policing of Families*, London: John Hopkins Press Ltd.

Emond, R. (2008) Children's Voices, Children's Rights. In Kendrick, A. (ed.) *Residential Child Care: Prospects and Challenges*, London: Jessica Kingsley, pp. 183–195.

Emond, R. (2003) Putting the care into residential care: the role of young people, *Journal of Social Work*, 3(3), 321–337.

Equality and Human Rights Commission (2009) *Staying on*, Published on 8 June 2009.

Farmer, E. and Pollock, S. (1998) *Sexually Abused and Abusing Children in Substitute Care*, Chichester: Wiley. Quoted in O'Neill, T. (2008) Gender Matters in Residential Child Care. In Kendrick, A. (ed.) *Residential Child Care: Prospects and Challenges*, London: Jessica Kingsley, pp.93–106.

Farrington, D. (1995) The Twelfth Jack Tizzard Memorial Lecture: the development of offending and antisocial behaviour from childhood: key findings from the Cambridge Study in Delinquent Development, *Journal of Child Psychology and Psychiatry*, 36, 253–268.

Fawcett, B., Featherstone, B. and Goddard, J. (2004) *Contemporary Child Care Policy and Practice*, Basingstoke: Palgrave Macmillan.

Fitzpatrick, C. (2009) Looked After Children and the Criminal Justice System. In Broadhurst, K., Grover, C. and Jamieson, J. (eds) *Critical Perspectives on Safeguarding Children*, Chichester: Wiley, pp.211–225.

Forrester, D., Goodman, G., Cocker, C., Binnie, C. and Jensch, G. (2007) *Does Care Work? A Focused Literature Review on Welfare Outcomes for Children Who Enter Care*, Welsh Assembly Government.

Foucault, M. (1978) *The History of Sexuality, Vol.1: An Introduction*, Harmondsworth: Penguin.

Foucault, M. (1977) *Discipline and Punish: The Birth of the Prison*, New York: Random House.

Francis, J. (2008) Could Do Better! Supporting the Education of Looked-after Children. In Kendrick, A. (ed.) *Residential Child Care: Prospects and Challenges*, London: Jessica Kingsley, pp.19–33.

Francis, J., Thomson, G.O.B. and Mills, S. (1996) *The Quality of Educational Experience of Children in Care*, Edinburgh: University of Edinburgh.

Frost, N., Mills, S. and Stein, M. (1999) *Understanding Residential Child Care*, Aldershot: Ashgate.

Goffman, E. (1961) *Asylums: Essays on the Social Situation of Mental Patients and Other Inmates*, New York: Doubleday.

Goldson, B. (2002) New Labour, social justice and children: political calculation and the deserving–undeserving schism, *British Journal of Social Work*, 32(6), 683–695.

Goldson, B. and Jamieson, J. (2002) Youth crime, the 'parenting deficit' and state intervention: a contextual critique, *Youth Justice*, 2(2), 82–99.

Goldson, B. and Muncie, J. (2006) Critical Anatomy: Towards a Principled Youth Justice. In Goldson, B. and Muncie, J. (eds) *Youth Crime and Justice: Critical Issues*, London: Sage.

Gottfredson, M.R. and Hirschi, T. (1990) *A General Theory of Crime*. Stanford, CA: Stanford University Press. Quoted in Muncie, J. (2004) *Youth and Crime* (2nd Edition), London: Sage.

Hancock, L. (2006) Urban Regeneration, Young People, Crime and Criminalisation In Goldson, B. and Muncie, J. (eds) *Youth Crime and Justice: Critical Issues*, London: Sage, pp.172–186.

Hannon, C., Wood, C. and Bazalgette, L. (2010) *To Deliver the Best for Looked after Children, the State Must be a Confident Parent: In Loco Parentis*, London: Demos.

Hayden, C. (2010) Offending behaviour in care: is children's residential care a 'criminogenic' environment? *Child and Family Social Work*, 15, 461–472.

Hayes, D. (2013) *Failing Children's Homes More than Double in a Year*, Children and Young People Now, www.cypnow.co.uk/cyp/news/1077606/failing-childrens-homes-double (URL last accessed on 27.8.13).

Hendrick, H. (2006) Histories of Youth Crime and Justice. In Goldson, B. and Muncie, J. (eds) *Youth Crime and Justice*, London: Sage, pp.3–16.

Heptinstall, E. (2000) Gaining access to looked after children for research purposes: lessons learned, *British Journal of Social Work*, 30(6), 867–872.

Hicks, L., Gibbs, I., Weatherley, H. and Byford, S. (2007) *Managing Children's Home's: Developing Effective Leadership in Small Organisations*, London: Jessica Kingsley.

Hirschi, T. (1969) *Causes of Delinquency*, Berkley: University of California Press. Quoted in Taylor, C. (2006) *Young People in Care and Criminal Behaviour*, London: Jessica Kingsley Publishers.

Home Office (1997) *No More Excuses– A New Approach to Tackling Youth Crime in England and Wales*, London: The Stationary Office.

Home Office (2004) *Preventative Approaches Targeting Young People in Local Authority Residential Care*, Home Office: London.

House of Commons (2011) *Looked-after Children: Further Government Response to the Third Report from the Children, Schools and Families Committee, Session 2008–9*, Education Committee, 4.4.2011, www.parliament.co.uk.

House of Commons Health Select Committee (1998) *Children Looked After by Local Authorities. (HC 319–1)*, London: The Stationary Office.

Howe, D. (2005) *Child Abuse and Neglect*, Hampshire: Palgrave Macmillan.

Huizinga, D., Schumann, K., Ehret, B. and Elliot, A. (2003) *The Effects of Juvenile Justice Processing on Subsequent Delinquent and Criminal Behaviour: A Cross-National Study*, Washington: Final report to the National Institute of Justice.

Jackson, S. (2006) Care Past and Present. In Chase, E., Simon, A. and Jackson, S. (eds) *In Care and After: A Positive Perspective*, London: Routledge.

Jonson-Reid, M. and Barth, R.P. (2000) From placement to prison: the path to adolescent incarceration from child welfare supervised foster or group care, *Children and Youth Services Review*, 22(7), 493–516.

Kendrick, A. (2012) What Research Tells Us about Residential Child Care. In Davies, M. (ed.) *Social Work with Children and Families*, Basingstoke: Palgrave Macmillan, pp.287–303.

Kendrick, A. (2008) Introduction: Residential Childcare. In Kendrick, A (ed.) *Residential Child Care: Prospects and Challenges*, London: Jessica Kingsley, pp.7–15.

Kendrick, A., Steckley, L. and McPheat, G.A. (2011) Residential Child Care: Learning from International Comparisons. In Taylor, R., Hill, M. and McNeill, F. (eds) *Early Professional Development for Social Workers*, Birmingham: Venture Press, pp.81–87.

Kilpatrick, R., Berridge, D., Sinclair, R., Larkin, E., Lucas, P.J., Kelly, B. and Geraghty, T. (2008) *Working with Challenging and Disruptive Situations in Residential Child Care: Sharing Effective Practice*, London: Social Care Institute for Excellence.

King, R., Raynes, N. and Tizzard, J. (1973) *Patterns of Residential Care*, London, Routledge and Kegan Paul. Quoted in Clough, R., Bullock, R. and Ward, A. (2006) *What Works in Residential Child Care: A Review of the Research Evidence and the Practical Considerations*, London: National Children's Bureau.

Layder, D. (2006) *Understanding Social Theory*, London: Sage.

Layder, D. (2004) *Emotion in Social Life: The Lost Heart of Society*, London: Sage.

Lea, J. and Young, J. (1984) *What is to be done about Law and Order?* Harmondsworth: Penguin. Quoted in Muncie, J. (2004) *Youth and Crime* (2nd Edition), London: Sage.

Leathers, S.J. (2002) Foster children's behavioural disturbance and detachment from caregivers and community institutions, *Children and Youth Services Review*, 24(4), 239–268.

Lee, R. (1993) *Doing Research on Sensitive Topics*, London: Sage. Quoted in Berridge, D. and Brodie, I. (1998) *Children's Homes Revisited*, London: Jessica Kingsley Publishers.

Lemert, E. (1967) *Human Deviance, Social Problems and Social Control*, Englewood Cliffs, NJ: Prentice Hall. Quoted in Muncie, J. (2004) *Youth and Crime* (2nd Edition), London: Sage.

Levitas, R. (2012*) There May be 'Trouble' Ahead: What We Know About these 120,000 'Troubled' Families*, Policy and Social Exclusion, UK, www.poverty. ac.uk/system/files/WP Policy Response No.3-'Trouble'ahead(LevitasFinal2 1April2012).pdf (URL last accessed 10.8.13).

Littlechild, B. and Sender, H. (2010) *The Introduction of Restorative Justice Approaches in Young People's Residential Units: A Critical Evaluation*, London: National Society for the Prevention of Cruelty to Children.

Magistrates Association (2012) Youth Courts Committee response to inquiry into the extent to which the youth justice system in England and Wales is fulfilling its principal aim of preventing offending by young people. Document number: 12/18, London, Justice Committee (http://www. magistrates-association.org.uk/dox/consultations/1333550424_youth_ justice_inquiry_response.pdf).

Martinson, R. (1974) What works? Questions and answers about prison reform, *The Public Interest*, 35, 22–54.

Masson, J. (2000) Legal Issues in Researching Children's Perspectives. In Lewis, A. and Lindsay, G. (eds) *Researching Children's Perspectives*, Buckingham: Open University Press, pp.34–45.

Matza, D. (1964) *Delinquency and Drift*, New York: Wiley. Quoted in Barry, M. (2006) *Youth Offending in Transition: The Search for Social Recognition*, Oxon: Routledge.

McAra, L. and McVie, S. (2010) Youth crime and justice: key messages from the Edinburgh study of youth transitions and crime, *Criminology and Criminal Justice*, 10(2), 179–209, Sage.

McAra, L. and McVie, S. (2007) 'Youth Justice' the impact of agency contact on desistance from offending', *European Journal of Criminology*, 4(3), 315–345.

McIntosh, I., Dorrer, N., Punch, S. and Emond, R. (2011) 'I Know We Can't Be a Family, But as Close as you Can Get': Displaying Families Within an Institutional Context. In Dermott, E. and Seymour, J. (eds) *Displaying Families: A New Concept for the Sociology of Family Life*, Basingstoke: Palgrave Macmillan.

McLeod, A. (2007) Whose agenda? issues of power and relationship when listening to looked after young people, *Child and Family Social Work*, 12(3), 278–286.

McNeill, F., Batchelor, S., Burnett, R. and Knox, J. (2005) *21st Century Social Work. Reducing Reoffending: Key Practice Skills*, Edinburgh, Scottish Executive. Quoted in Barry, M. (2007) *Risk Assessment in Criminal Justice: The Challenge for Inter-Agency Cooperation*. Paper presented to 2007 Social Sciences Conference, Granada.

McCann, J.B., James, A., Wilson, S. and Dunn, G. (1996) Prevalence of psychiatric disorders in young people in the care system, *British Medical Journal* 313, 1529–1530.

McNeish, D., Newman, T. and Roberts, H. (2002) *What Works for Children?* Buckingham: Open University Press.

Meltzer, H., Lader, D., Corbin, T., Goodman, R. and Ford, T. (2004) *The Mental Health of Young People Looked After by Local Authorities in Scotland.* London, TSO. Quoted in Van Bienum, M. (2008) Mental Health and Children and Young People in Residential Care. In Kendrick, A. (ed.) *Residential Child Care: Prospects and Challenges,* London: Jessica Kingsley, pp.47–59.

Ministry of Justice (MoJ) (2013) Youth Cautions–Guidance for Police and Youth Offending Teams, Crown Copyright, www.justice.gov.uk/downloads/oocd/youth-cautions-guidance-police-yots-oocd.pdf (URL last accessed on 4.5.13).

Ministry of Justice (MOJ) (2012) *Women and the Criminal Justice System,* www.justice.gov.uk/statistics/criminal-justice/women (updated 22.11.12) (URL last accessed on 9.2.13).

Ministry of Justice (MoJ) (2010) Breaking the Cycle: *Effective Punishment, Rehabilitation and Sentencing of Offenders,* Crown Copyright, www.justice.gov.uk.

Ministry of Justice/Youth Justice Board (MoJ/YJB) (2012) *Youth Justice Statistics: England and Wales 2010/12,* www-justice.gov.uk/publications/youth-justice-statistics.htm (URL last accessed on 9.2.13)

Mitchell, J. (1983) 'Case study and situational analysis', *Sociological Review,* 31, 187–211.

Morgan, D.L. (1988) *Focus Groups as Qualitative Research,* London: Sage. Quoted in Wilkinson, S. (1999) How Useful are Focus Groups in Feminist Research? In Barbour, S. and Kitzinger, J. (eds) *Developing Focus Group Research–Politics, Theory and Practice,* London: Sage, pp.64–78.

Morgan, R. (2011) *Messages for Munro: A Report of Children's Views Collected for Professor Eileen Munro by the Children's Rights Director for England,* Manchester: Ofsted.

Morgan, R. (2009) *Life in Children's Homes: A Report of Children's Experience,* London: Ofsted.

Morgan, R. (2007) *Leeds University Centre for Criminal Justice Studies Annual Lecture* given on 8 May 2007.

Morgan, R. (2006) *'Your Rights! Your Say'. Children's Views on Standards: A Children's Views Report,* London: Commission for Social Care Inspection.

Morris, S. and Wheatley, H. (1994) *Time to Listen: The Experience of Young People in Foster and Residential Care,* London: Childline.

Muncie, J. and Goldson, B. (2006) England and Wales: The New Correctionalism. In Muncie, J. and Goldson, B. (eds) *Comparative Youth Justice: Critical Issues,* London: Sage.

Muncie, J. (2004) *Youth and Crime* (2nd Edition), London: Sage.

Muncie, J. (2000) *Pragmatic Realism? Searching for Criminology.* In Goldson, B. (ed.) *The New Youth Justice,* Lyme Regis: Russell House Publishing, pp.33–44.

Munro, E. (2011) The Munro Review of Child Protection: Final Report A Child-Centred System, https://www.gov.uk/government/uploads/system/uploads/attachment_data/file/175391/Munro-Review.pdf (URL last accessed on 24.8.13).

Munro, E. and Hardy, A. (2007) *Placement Stability: A Review of the Literature*, Loughborough: Loughborough University.

Nacro (2012) *Reducing Offending by Looked After Children*, London: Nacro.

Nacro (2009) *Some Facts about Children and Young People Who Offend 2007: Youth Crime Briefing*, March, London: NACRO. .

Nacro (2005) *A Handbook on Reducing Offending by Looked After Children*, London: Nacro.

Nacro (2003) *Reducing Offending by Looked after Children: Good Practice Guide*, London: Nacro.

National Care Association (2009) *Every Budget Matters: A Survey of the Current Commissioning Practices and the Health of the Residential Child Care Sector*, London.

Nayak, A. (2003) *Race, Place and Globalization: Youth Cultures in a Changing World*, Oxford: Berg.

Ofsted (2013) *Inspection of Services for Children in Need of Help and Protection, Children Looked After and Care Leavers: Consultation Document*, 14 June 2013, www.ofsted.gov.uk/resources/inspection-of-services-for-children-need-of-help-and-protection-children-looked-after-and-care-leave. (URL last accessed on 24.8.2013).

Ofsted (2011) *Edging Away from Care: How Services Successfully Prevent Young People Entering Care*, Manchester: Ofsted.

O'Neill, T. (2008) Gender Matters in Residential Child Care. In Kendrick, A. (ed.) *Residential Child Care: Prospects and Challenges*, London: Jessica Kingsley, pp.93–106.

O'Sullivan, T. (2011) *Decision Making in Social Work* (2nd edition), Hampshire: Palgrave Macmillan.

Packman, J. and Hall, C. (1998) *From Care to Accommodation: Support, Protection and Control in Child Care Services*, London: Stationary Office.

Packman, J., Randall, J. and Jacques, N. (1986) *Who Needs Care?* Oxford: Blackwell. Quoted in Smith, R. (2009) Childhood, Agency and Youth Justice, *Children and Society*, 23(4), 252–264.

Pawson, R. and Tilley, N. (1997) *Realistic Evaluation*, London: Sage.

Pemberton, C. (2013) The Children's Services Blog, Community Care, 14.6.13, http://www.communitycare.co.uk/blogs/childrens-services-blog/2013/06/ofsted-to-replace-good-inspection-rating-with-new-requires-improve-ment-rating/#.UgPWAGoGV4 (URL last accessed 7.8.13).

Pemberton, C. (2011) Third of councils no longer run children's homes. Community Care, 14 September 2011, http://www.communitycare.co.uk/Articles/14/09/2011/117438/third-of-councils-no-longer-run-or-own-children's-homes.htm.

Piachaud, D. (2005) Child Poverty: An Overview. In Preston, G. (ed.) *At Greatest Risk: The Children Most Likely to be Poor*, London: Child Poverty Action Group.

Piachaud, D. (2001) Child poverty, opportunities and quality of life, *The Political Quarterly*, 72(4), 446–453.

Pickford, J. and Dugmore, P. (2012) *Youth Justice and Social Work* (2nd Edition), London: Sage.

Pitts, J. (2003) Youth Justice in England and Wales. In Matthews, R. and Young, J. (eds) *The New Politics of Crime and Punishment*, Devon: Willan, pp.71–99.

Polsky, H.W. (1962) *Cottage Six: the Social System of Delinquent Boys in Residential Treatment*, New York: Russell Sage.

Prison Reform Trust (2008) *Criminal Damage: Why We Should Lock up Fewer Children*, London: Prison Reform Trust.

Puffett, N. (2014) *U-turn Over Process for Long-distance Care Placements*, www. cypnow.co.uk (URL last accessed 7.1.14)

Rose, J. (2002) *Working with Young People in Secure Accommodation: From Chaos to Culture*, Hove: Bruner-Routledge.

Rutherford, A. (1992) *Growing Out of Crime: The New Era*, Winchester: Waterside Books.

Rutter, M., Giller, H. and Hagell, A. (1998) *Antisocial Behaviour by Young People*, Cambridge: Cambridge University Press.

Schofield, G. (2003) *Part of the Family: Pathways Through Foster Care*, London: BAAF.

Schofield, G., Ward, E., Biggart, L., Scaife, V., Dodsworth, J., Larsson, B., Haynes, A. and Stone, N. (2012) *Looked After Children and Offending: Reducing Risk and Promoting Resilience: Executive Summary*, East Anglia: University of East Anglia.

Scourfield, P. (2007) Are there reasons to be worried about the 'cartelisation' of residential care? *Critical Social Policy*, 27(2), 155–181. Quoted in Smith, M. (2009a) *Rethinking Residential Child Care-Positive Perspectives*, Bristol: Policy Press.

Shaw, J. and Frost, N. (2013) *Young People and the Care Experience: Research, Policy and Practice*, Sussex: Routledge.

Silver, D. (2012) *The Social Justice Strategy: Transforming Lives for the Better?* http://www.theguardian.com/uk/the-northerner/2012/mar/19/reading-the-riots-blogpost-salford-manchester-social-justice (URL last accessed 30.12.13).

Sinclair, I. and Gibbs, I. (1998) *Children's Homes: A Study in Diversity*, Chichester: Wiley.

Smith, M. (2009a) *Rethinking Residential Child Care-Positive Perspectives*, Bristol: Policy Press.

Smith, R. (2009b) Childhood, agency and youth justice, *Children and Society*, 23(4), 252–264.

Smith, R. (2007) *Youth Justice: Ideas, Policy, Practice*, Cullompton: Willan.

Smith, D. (2000) Learning from the Scottish juvenile justice system, *Probation Journal*, 47(1), 12–17.

Soloman, E. and Garside, R. (2008) *Ten Years of Labour's Youth Justice Reforms: An Independent Audit*, London: Centre for Crime and Justice Studies, www. crimeandjustice.org.

Stein, M. (2006) Wrong turn, *The Guardian*, Wednesday 6 December.

Stein, M., Rees, G., Hicks, L. and Gorin, S. (2009) Neglected Adolescents-Literature Review (Summary). https://www.education.gov.uk/publications/

standard/publicationdetail/page1/DCSF-RBX-09–04 Quoted in Berridge, D., Biehal, N. and Henry, L. (2012) *Living in Children's Residential Homes* (Research Report), London: Department for Education.

Stevens, I. and Furnivall, J. (2008) Therapeutic Approaches in Residential Child Care. In Kendrick, A (ed.) *Residential Child Care: Prospects and Challenges*, London: Jessica Kingsley, pp.196–209.

Stewart, J., Smith, D., Stewart., G. and C. Fullwood (1994) *Understanding Offending Behaviour*, Harlow, Essex: Longman Group Limited. Quoted in Taylor, C. (2005) *Young People in Care and Criminal Behaviour*, London: Jessica Kingsley.

Strauss, A.L. and Corbin, J. (1998) *Basics of Qualitative Research: Techniques and Procedures for Developing Grounded Theory*, CA: Sage.

Such, E. and Walker, R. (2005) Young citizens or policy objects? children in the 'rights and responsibilities' debate, *Journal of Social Policy*, 34(1), 39–58. Quoted in Smith, R. (2009b) Childhood, Agency and Youth Justice, *Children and Society*, 23(4), 252–264.

Sutherland, H., Sefton, D. and Piachaud, D. (2003) *Poverty in Britain: The Impact of Government Policy Since 1997*, York: Joseph Rowntree Foundation.

Taylor, C. (2006) *Young People in Care and Criminal Behaviour*, London: Jessica Kingsley Publishers.

The Adolescent and Children's Trust (TACT) (2008) *Care Experience and Criminalisation– An Executive Summary.*

The Children's Partnership (2013) *Summary Briefing: Children and Families Bill Amendments to Children's Home Regulation*, www.thechildrenspartnership-knowledge.org.uk/media/1017/13311/childrens–homes–regulations–final.pdf (URL last accessed 1.1.14).

The Who Cares Trust (2013) *Extension of Foster Care to 21 and the Implications for Residential Care*, www.thewhocarestrust.org.uk.

Tickle, L. (2012) *Looked-after Children: Care Should be in the Community, The Guardian Professional*, Wednesday 24 October, 2012.

Topping, A. (2013) *Michael Gove Attacks Lack of Transparency in Children's Homes*, The Guardian, 13.9.13, www.theguardian.com/society/2013/sep/13/michael-gove-transparency-childrens-homes (URL last accessed 13.9.13).

Tracy, P.E. and Kempf-Leonard (1996) *Continuity and Discontinuity in Criminal Careers*, New York: Plenum.

Ungar, M. (2000) The myth of peer pressure, *Adolescence*, 35(137), Spring, 167–180.

Utting, W. (1997) *People Like Us*, The Report of the Review of the Safeguards for Children Living Away from Home, London: The Stationary Office.

Van Bienum, M. (2008) Mental Health and Children and Young People in Residential Care. In Kendrick, A. (ed.) *Residential Child Care: Prospects and Challenges*, London: Jessica Kingsley, pp.47–59.

Wade, J. and Biehal, N. with Stein, M. and Clayden, J. (1998) *Going Missing*, Chichester: Wiley.

Waiton, S. (2001) *Adult Recognition of Adolescent Peer Relations*. Paper presented at the Strathclyde Youth Conference, Glasgow. Quoted in Barry, M. (2006)

Youth Offending in Transition: The Search for Social Recognition, Oxon: Routledge.

Ward, A. (2000) Opportunity led work, Paper presented at the first Annual Conference of the Scottish Institute for Residential Child Care, Glasgow, 4 June 2000.

Ward, H., Holmes, L. and Soper, J. (2008) *Costs and Consequences of Placing Children in Care*, London: Jessica Kingsley.

Ward, H. and Skuse, T. (2001) Performance targets and stability of placements for children being looked after away from home. *Children and Society*, 15, 333–346. Quoted in Taylor, C. (2006) *Young People in Care and Criminal Behaviour*, London: Jessica Kingsley.

Warner, N. (1992) *Choosing with Care*. The Report of the Committee of Inquiry into the Selection, Development and Management of Staff in Children's Homes, London: HMSO.

Waterhouse, R. (2000) *Lost in Care*: Report of the Tribunal of Inquiry into the Abuse of Children in Care in the former County Council Areas of Gwynedd and Clwyd since 1974, London: HMSO.

Webster, C. (2006) 'Race' Youth Crime and Justice. In Goldson, B. and Muncie, J. (eds) *Youth Crime and Justice: Critical Issues*, London: Sage, pp.30–46.

Whitaker, D, Archer, L and Hicks, L. (1998) *Working in Children's Homes: Challenges and Complexities*, Chichester: Wiley.

White, J.T., Moffitt, T.E., Earls, F., Robins, L. and Silva, P.A. (1990) How early can we tell? predictors of childhood conduct disorder and adolescent delinquency *Criminology*, 28(4), 507–533.

White, R. and Cunneen, C. (2006) Social Class, Youth Crime and Justice. In Goldson, B. and Muncie, J. (eds) *Youth Crime and Justice: Critical Issues*, London: Sage, pp.17–29.

Wiggins, K. (2013) Ofsted inspection plan branded 'inadequate', local government chronicle (LGC), www.lgcplus.com/briefings/services/children-services/ofsted-inspection-plan-branded-inadequate/5061087.article, (URL last accessed on 24.8.2013).

Wilkinson, R.G. and Pickett, K. (2009) *The Spirit Level*, Harmondsworth: Allen Lane.

Willmott, N. (2007) *A Review of the Use of Restorative Justice in Children's Residential Care*, London: National Children's Bureau.

Wilson, J.Q. and Herrnstein, R.J. (1985) *Crime and Human Nature*. New York: Simon and Schuster. Quoted in Muncie, J. (2004) *Youth and Crime* (2nd Edition), London: Sage.

Wilson, J.Q. (1975) *Thinking About Crime*, Basic Books: New York.

Winnett, R. (2013) 'Borstal' plans for young offenders, *The Telegraph*, 13 February 2013, http://www.telegraph.co.uk (URL last accessed on 16.06.13).

Worsley, R. (2006) *Young People in Custody 2004–2006: An Analysis of Children's Experiences of Prison*, London: HMIP and YJB.

Yin, R.K. (1994) *Case Study Research: Design and Methods* (2nd Edition) London: Sage.

YJB (2013) Monthly Youth Custody Report–February 2013, http://www. justice.gov.uk/statistics/youth-justice/custody-data.

YJB and MoJ (2012) Youth Justice Statistics 2010/11 England and Wales, www. justice.gov.uk/publications/youth-justice-statistics.htm (URL last accessed on 26.1.12).

Index

Lightning Source UK Ltd.
Milton Keynes UK
UKOW06n2240290116